ECOPRENEURING
Managing for Results

I am more than a little committed to this process personally and more committed to your success than you know. I realize it is possible to accomplish and do and be what you want. I wish you well.

> Richard James Blue

ECOPRENEURING
Managing for Results

Richard James Blue

Scott, Foresman and Company
Glenview, Illinois   London

ISBN 0-673-46005-3

Copyright © 1990 Richard James Blue.
All Rights Reserved.
Printed in the United States of America.

Library of Congress Cataloging-in-Publication Data

Blue, Richard James.
  Ecopreneuring : managing for results / Richard James Blue.
    p. cm.
  ISBN 0-673-46005-3
  1. Management. I. Title.
HD38.B626 1990   89-37021
658.4—dc20   CIP

1 2 3 4 5 6 MPC 94 93 92 91 90 89

Scott, Foresman professional books are available for bulk sales at quantity discounts. For information, please contact Marketing Manager, Professional Books Group, Scott, Foresman and Company, 1900 East Lake Avenue, Glenview, IL 60025.

To

Ruth Marion and James William

for life and the belief that anything is possible

to

Joseph, Everett, Evelyn, Claire, Eleanor, Shirley, Geraldine

and

Evelyn, James, Francis, Marilyn, Robert, Madeline

and

Ruth

for preceding me and in doing so created my life's opportunities

to

Murph, Miss Hubbard, the Marderosians, Ranger Farrell, Bill Cavanaugh,
Sam Labate, Howard, Paul Dube, Gene Blackman, Edith Olds, Roland Moody,
Bob Green, Lil Rogers, Irv Sands, Bob Palmer, Dick Conlon, Irv Pollitt,
Hal Pearson, Carolyn Williamson, John Kris, Dick Young, Edwin Land,
Bill McCune, Milton Green, Bill Uranek, Viola Saltmarsh, Hope Rossi,
John Mitchell, Leonard Meade, Burtrom Hollawell, Margie Ives, Gene Carter,
Frank Lennon, Margaret Booker, Rod Smith, Donald MacLean, Bob Minton,
Pat Fitzgerald, Chris Reagan, Liz Cappazoli, Florence Bracket, Harry Joel,
Dan McCarthy, Jack Denise, John Stockwell, Chris Culter, Barbara Reiman,
Carol LeDuc, Mal Campbell, Bob Shelnutt, Oliver Scott, Bruce Warren,
Janet Menn, Elaine Landry-Pion, Karen Scbinico, Steve Quigley, Jim Dolph,
Vic Morano, Peg Horrigan, Ted Kelley, Shirley Stretch, Paul Downey,
Fran Lipson, Jennifer Moorin, Ted Zeller, Debbie Gogliettino, Alan Lewis,
Bruce Washburn, Bruce Epstein, Jean McCormick, Val Gilman, Lori Henry,
Lori Corron, Richard LeMay, Betty McGee, Bob Jacobson, John LaTassa,
Paul Bascom, Mark Campbell, Ellie Hayes, Fran Charles, Henry Lewis,
Lorraine LaCombe, Larry Loomis, Clayton Lafferty and Human Synergistics, and
countless others

for their thoughts, words and actions, all of which have contributed
immeasurably to my growth and understanding.

to

Pamela, Sarah, Judith and Tom

for both the essence of tomorrow and the existence of today

and to

Jennifer

who, as my soul mate, is the source of love's passion and life's potential

Contents

   Introduction 1

1 Ecopreneur 7

2 Challenges 10

3 Ownership 14

4 People 32

5 Work 38

6 Business Ecology/Environment 44
    Catalysts 44
      Ownership 45
      Technology and Marketing 47
      Product or Market Driven 49
      Geographics and Demographics 51
      Work Force 53
      Fiscal 54
      Summary 56
    Developmental Stages 57
      Start-Up—The Concentration Is Energy 58
      Foothold—The Concentration Is Expertise 60

Niche—The Concentration Is Emotion   61
Image—The Concentration Is Ego   63
Potential—The Concentration Is Exposure   66
Summary   68

Management Stages   69
Group Process   69
Creation—Introduction   70
Structure—Role Definition   73
Actions and Reactions   75
Integrated Management   77
Summary   79

7 Individual and Organizational Needs   80

Job and Fair Pay/Stable and Trained Work Force   83
People—Job and Fair Pay   83
Company—Stable and Trained Work Force   83

Performance Standards/Maximum Productivity   86
People—Performance Standards   86
Company—Maximum Productivity   89

Productivity Assessment   91

Participation/Control   98
People—Participation   98
Company—Control   99

Recognition/Structure   102
People—Recognition   102
Company—Structure   103

Growth/Planning   108
People—Growth   108
Company—Planning   109
Summary   111

8 Management Ecopreneurial Technology   113

Management Styles   114
Authoritative/Custodial/Participative   118
Summary   138

Management Conflict   138
Summary   143

Management Stress   143
Summary   149

9 Management Ecopreneurial Strategies   151

The Perception Level   152
  Eco-challenges and Ego-challenges   152
  Company Stress and Personal Stress   156
  Management Behavior   167
  Management Communications   170
  Personal Communication   174
  Management Time   178
The Practical Level   184
  Defining the Job   184
  Developing Performance Standards   188
  Goal Setting   193
The Attitudinal Level   204

Index   207

Introduction

This is a book to assist you in being successful in your work environment. It will show you the skills, characteristics, attitudes, behaviors, and styles of successful people at the managerial and supervisory levels of responsibility in small to medium-size organizations. The average manager or supervisor works for a company that is not like the big companies in either size or disposition. The ownership of these smaller companies is in direct and often constant contact with the momentary, hourly, daily, weekly, and monthly operations of the company. Small and medium-size companies are different from the conglomerates often used as examples in management books. This book will display a work world that is like the one in which you live. You will be able to recognize what makes a manager successful, assess the degree to which you have similar skills and abilities, and develop a plan that will enable you to implement any necessary changes. Although I will often describe optimal environments, your work environment most likely will be little or nothing like the optimal one. The question this book is designed to answer is, "How can you be successful if your work environment is far from perfect?"

Do not look for a concise list of winning companies. This book is not about companies. It is about people in companies.

This year's award-winning company is next year's problem. The difference is the people who manage the company. A company with positive intent and inadequate managers is a losing company. On the other hand, a company with indifferent intent and good managers can be a winning company. The difference is in the nature and competency of the managers. Books that focus on companies and not on the individual managers are missing the point.

PREMISE

1. There are specific strategies needed to manage the given circumstances of modern organizations and succeed in middle and upper management.

2. Managers continue to be frustrated by experts who tell them the solution is in major change to an environment over which they have little or no control.

3. Managers need skills in management styles, management stress, management conflict, and management time. Each of these is specific and unique to managers. The process is proactive when it is effective. In other words, managers create the stimulus for others rather than simply responding to the inherent environmental stimuli. To take a program or a course or to read a book on stress management, conflict management, or time management suggests a reaction to stress, conflict, and time. Stress, conflict, and time are not necessarily negative. Oppression and manipulation are negative. Being out of control is negative. Indifference is negative.

4. This book refers to management style, not style management. There are styles that are appropriate to middle and upper management, not all the elements of which are seen as positive. Knowing the assets and liabilities of each is empowering and enables managers to use management stress, management conflict, and management time. Purposefully fitting the right style to the actual demands of the job is essential.

5. This book refers to management stress, not stress man-

agement. To manage is to create stress. Knowing what kinds are effective and positive is crucial.

6. This book refers to management conflict, not conflict management. To manage is to be in conflict. Understanding conflict and using its energy, not its force, develops organizational power.

7. This book refers to management time, not time management. Managers don't manage time, they manage their actions. If they were actually managing time, they could slow down, speed up, or even stop time.

The average manager works for a small or medium-size company—about 500 employees. He or she is eager to be successful. These managers read books that bombard the reader with the obvious. After reading these books, the managers would like to send all owners and CEOs to *In Search of Excellence*'s Tom Peters for a brain transplant. That's what it would take. They know their bosses can't seem to implement the ideas on their own, so they assume that any significant change is unlikely. Interestingly, it is from the middle and upper management personnel that this change will come, despite the limited power at these levels. They have people above them who, with a single word, can squelch an idea they have developed, nurtured, and presented.

According to the *Statistical Abstract of the United States: 1988* (U.S. Department of Commerce, Bureau of the Census, 108th edition),

- In 1984, 16 million businesses filed tax returns. The breakdown of those businesses was as follows:
    11.2 million were sole proprietorships
    1.6 million were partnerships
    3.2 million were corporations
- In that same year, of the 113.5 million in the labor force, there were 105 million people employed, which breaks down as follows:
    16 million worked for the government (federal, state, local, etc.)

11 million were self-employed or military personnel
78 million worked for all other employers
- Nearly 80 percent of the 78 million who worked for all other employers, or 62 million people, worked for companies that employed fewer than 500 employees.

It is clear from these numbers that the average person is influenced by ownership that is either a single person or a small group of partners.

Figure 1

Although the data is not sufficiently clear to determine the number of supervisors and managers, it appears that of the 62 million about one in twenty is a supervisor. There are approximately 3 million managers and supervisors who manage in environments that are nothing like the companies that employ the other 20 percent and get the spotlight, such as Ford, Westinghouse, 3M, Digital Equipment Corporation, and Polaroid, to name a few.

The current books on the market are frustrating managers by focusing on large companies, which are a good reference for only one person in five. This book is designed to demonstrate how successful managers operate in their actual circumstances. Successful managers find that the boss is open to change when managers show they can produce. The question is, which comes first, the chicken or the egg? The chicken is the organization's essence or nature, as defined by the ownership, and the egg is the organization's effectiveness. The former is ultimately in the hands of the owners/operators and the latter is in the hands of the management. All managers know who has the power. This book will enable managers to manage for results while the slow wheels of change grind away.

1
Ecopreneur

This book is based on the nature and style of *ecopreneurs*. They are winners. They are not born; they develop specific skills and use a view of the world that enables them to extract the positive aspects of each situation or circumstance in order to grow. They know they work for themselves and their goals, often in an environment controlled by someone else. They take the environment they get and change what can be changed, accept what can't be changed, and know it doesn't take a genius to tell the difference. The change must be in the way one works with the environment one gets. In the very same environment, the loser (unskilled manager) will go in one direction, and the ecopreneur (skillful manager) will go in another.

Throughout this book I will use the term *ecology* in the sense of the circumstances, the pressures, and the requirements placed on people in their work environment. This can sometimes be the way people at the top, the ownership of the organization, treat people, respond to them, or ignore them. It can also have clear connection to the expectations that are placed on people. Working in an environment where zero defect is the expectation, or where people are expected to produce their best, leads to tension. Tension is a natural condition in any ecology. However, there are several ways to react to tension. One specific reaction, the most common for those who manage poorly, is to convert tension to contention. These managers are competing against others, specifically resisting the organization as it is. This is clearly a reactive relationship to the environment. Since it is reactive most people feel as though they are not in control. This lack of control tends to lead people to negative attitudes. Those negative attitudes lead to an overwhelming physical exhaustion at the end of the day, and ultimately leads people to feel distress in their work.

Another way to respond to tension is to convert it, as the ecopreneurs do, into intention, or establishing and working with goals, aims, and guides. They work toward something as opposed to working against something.

It is important to do one's best, not necessarily to achieve the impossible, but to be able to count yourself as one who has met the test by bringing out your best effort. This way there is a feeling there are actions rather than reactions. This leads to a feeling of control, and with control, power is transformed into energy. That energy brings with it a sense of physical connectedness and alertness, which leads to positive attitudes and a feeling of success. Thus, when these attitudes are brought together, the ecopreneur experiences a feeling of positive stress and nearly boundless energy, which have been created out of tension.

There is an ecostructure greenhouse effect putting heat on the American work environment. There is a need for significant change. The change must come in the way we work with the environments we get. This book is dedicated to those who have learned to survive and grow (ecopreneurs) and to those who are eager to learn, who are in the fray, who know they can't change anything in any dramatic way, and who are frustrated by books that tell them the solution to their problems is to change their environment. This book is for those who are looking for ways to make it work in their present circumstances. They will learn to build integrated teams by using management stress, management conflict, management communications, and management time instead of reacting to them.

The stream of ecopreneurial consciousness flows inexorably from one's goals. The ecopreneurs are those who, in a changing environment of political tension and conflicting and confusing initiatives with ownership and leadership that is apathetic or aggressive and inept or competent, assure the future through goals supported by organizational structure. They also have control of resources for maximum results (productivity) through quality performance of a stable and trained work force.

2
Challenges

Primary Goal:
> To describe the nature of the challenge process to be used in this book and to introduce the reader to the question of determination

Intermediate Objectives:
> To establish the relationship I wish to have with you as you read this book
>
> To introduce Eco-Challenges
>
> To introduce Ego-Challenges
>
> To describe how the information will be used

You will have the opportunity to relate your organization to ideal organizational ecostructures, and your actions, attitudes, beliefs, and commitments to successful ecopreneurs. The ideal company exists only as a theoretical model. I do not define it in order for you to judge your company as good or bad but rather as a way to assess the nature and degree of the ecological pressures acting on you and to which you are reacting. Neither is the presentation of the nature of successful ecopreneurs designed to prove them right and you wrong in order for you to feel imperfect. You will have the opportunity to make a determination of the degree to which you reflect the behavior and attitudes of an ecopreneur and to see if you have the determination to alter your behavior and attitudes. The word *determination* is used intentionally because of the double meaning—to make a determination and to have determination. You will have the opportunity throughout this book to discover whether you are determined to rise above your circumstances or if you are going to be determined by your circumstances. The objective is threefold: (1) to have you look at the areas where there seem to be significant differences between you and ecopreneurs, (2) to consider alternative behaviors and points of view, and (3) to implement change if you see both logic and value in doing so.

All the effective behaviors of ecopreneurs should pass the test of being patently obvious when examined. The only reason you wouldn't have put them into practice is because you didn't know how. I will show you how in the strategy section of this book. It is important to me that you not accept anything that isn't completely sensible to you. All the effective behavior of ecopreneurs should pass that test. If you see a need for change in your approach and choose not to do it, it should be because it doesn't require attention at this moment or that your current technique is working. I don't see myself as the teacher or you as the students. My goal is for you to observe what your senses know to be true and report truth in a way that provides opportunity for you to fulfill your potential as managers and to present the solutions to the problems of implementation that successful managers have found effective.

I will describe many positive and supportive lessons that organizations can learn from the many influences on their environments. This is not done to enable you to grade your company as good or bad, but rather to confirm the presence or absence of these influences as either a support or something to be worked through. It is an opportunity to see what you may be allowing to get in your way and what ecopreneurs don't let stop them. Ecopreneurs don't only emerge from well-run organizations with positive environments and ecologies. It is precisely because they can and do come out of seriously flawed work environments that I have written this book and it is the basis for its optimistic point of view.

The successful behavior of ecopreneurs can be defined and copied. The effective management and organizational behavior of companies, not as they should be, but as they are, can also be defined. Managers will be able to assess themselves and their organizations to determine the degree to which they are resisting the natural character of their organizations. As you go through the remainder of this book, you will have the opportunity to rate your company on **eco-challenges** and yourself on **ego-challenges**. The eco-challenges will enable you to rate your company on its basic ecological state, structure, and development. Obviously, the ego-challenges have to do with you. You will rate yourself against the styles, behaviors, characteristics, and skills of the people who seem to be the most adept at managing in environments that range from hostile to supportive. The rating scale is from three to nine.

3	4	5	6	7	8	9

You need only to put an X in any one of the seven spaces. Each end of the scale will be defined. The definitions might be:

    3 — The people who work for me are meeting none of their productivity potentials. They are basically unconscious to productivity issues.

    to

    9 — The people who work for me are meeting all of their productivity potentials and are constantly aware of productivity improvements.

When we have finished the descriptive and diagnostic part of the book you will be given an opportunity to collect all the data from these challenges, rate yourself and your company, determine a plan of action, and define specific strategies to accomplish your objectives. Since you can control yourself to a much greater extent than you can control your company, more focus will be given to you and your needs, actions, and strategies. The assessment of the company is to establish the context for your actions. I promise I will not tell you to change anything over which you have no control in order to be successful.

3

Ownership

Primary Goal:
> To describe ownership, top management, and CEOs across a broad and acceptable range of behavior

Intermediate Objectives:
> To describe commonplace circumstances at work
>
> To present a range of demeanors prevalent in the people at the top of organizations
>
> To demonstrate how work comes to people
>
> To evidence that too much to do is the norm

The nature of an organization is determined largely by the leadership, ownership, CEO—the boss. People at the top differ greatly in their style, approach, and concerns. I have known dozens of people who were clear on their way to the top that they would not be like so many already at the top—arrogant, power-hungry, win-fixated, and apparently uncaring. Many are at the top now and have become precisely what they said they would not. There is something about the job at the top, something about politics, something about only appearing to be at the top, something about winning for everyone, and something about going home daily with the jobs and livelihoods of several hundred people influenced by your decisions that changes people.

The totally unnatural circumstances of the workplace operate on each of us differently. Some take to it with a warmth and humanism we somehow expect is needed. Others operate out of force and the need to win at everything, competing and contrary to a fault. What is true is that they are all capable of bringing out the big guns when things get tough or when the survival of the organization is at stake. There is considerable evidence that if they are unwilling to adopt this behavior the survival of the organization is even more in peril.

This point was made by Michael, a CEO, in a recent training program I was directing, which was designed to enhance management skills in performance evaluation, quality, and productivity. (I try not to include CEOs in training for skill development because most can't actually understand what is required to identify performance standards, measure them, and give feedback.) I had just finished describing the model of rational performance standards. That is, tell people you want perfect results (i.e., every customer is satisfied every time) unless there are barriers in their way (i.e., parts break down, unclear customer expectations, incompetent co-workers), in which case they are expected to take all appropriate actions to minimize the effect of the barriers. Michael's eyes shot up from the table in front of him. He had just heard something that rang totally discordant to him. There are no barriers, just challenges. He saw the idea of barriers the same as excuses. He knew his performance was to be measured on results and his superiors did not care about his barriers.

It may be important to know that he was the third of four presidents of this division of the company in a period of six or seven years. This might help you understand the nature of the pressures and expectations he was living with. For him the idea of success was to win or he would be gone. The people in the room were many of his direct reports and he was concerned that they might be affected by this clearly wimpy approach to quality and performance. I am clear that the only way to measure performance is to take into account both results and effort and I was not prepared to alter my message to suit his views.

It was time for lunch and so we broke on that note. I sought him out during lunch and found him in his office. I told him that we should stop the training at that point if he had serious concerns about the basis of my approach to quality and performance. For a reason not clear to me and I would guess to this day still not clear to him, we continued the program. He said he had grave disagreements with the idea of barriers as points of reference to discuss performance. This is an attitude that one should expect from a person who is both under the gun to perform or else, and whose natural style is to operate from power and a need to win every time. We did continue. We never did overcome his objections.

In the end, it is all irrelevant. The people who make it work are the managers. Michael was blind to the nature of reason that I applied to the issues. What I presented is logical and rational. He lives in an illogical, irrational, and political world and cannot see the value in looking at anything but the goal. All the rest is incidental and that's the way a president should think. He is the visionary, and he must think anything is possible.

His immediate subordinates know the only way to maximize quality and performance is to minimize the effects of the barriers. He told a story with great pride during the training. When he took over the organization the turnaround time on returned products from unsatisfied customers used to be several weeks and now it was down to five or six days. His enthusiasm around this achievement was considerable. It was also clear that his senior and middle managers in that department had had to overcome many obstacles to accomplish this feat. He gave them considerable credit for their results. He simply isn't interested in the effort. He has a management perspective much like Lee Iacocca's, which is firmly focused on energy, enthusiasm, possibilities, and the future. That makes him a poor manager of the present, but that's all right, it's not his job. His managers must function well in environments where priorities will be unclear (he wants it all, now), where little rewards are given for a well-run race, and where there will be little feedback except on what isn't happening.

People who lead from this position characteristically need to win, and you have their support as long as you contribute to their win. If you stop, they will make your life miserable. Not directly but by including you out. They will tell you that you have their unqualified support but when you screw up you will be all alone to face the consequences. Associating with things or people that aren't working out is a deterrent to maintaining an attitude where anything is possible. In the long run, the success of the organization may well require this duality. After all, this person is responsible for the livelihood of hundreds of people and your petty issues (barriers) pale in comparison.

This is neither uncommon nor is it wrong. It is simply one of the many variations of management from the top. For the senior and middle managers, it is a barrier which they must handle in order to get their jobs done. It is a major element in the ecology of a company. If the senior and middle management don't transform the message as it goes to people further down and give credit for effort, there may be turnover of the people the company can least afford to lose, the winners. Michael is typical of many of the people who hold down the job of CEO. He doesn't see himself as typical and on a lot of levels he is not. His management view is extremely commonplace, which is why he is a good model and included in this book. I just wouldn't buy a book he would write on how to manage.

Buck is the president of a small (about $30 to $40 million in annual sales), fast-growing service company. He is the president and the majority owner. He is extremely bright, egocentric, and dominant. Apparently, he thinks nothing of yelling and ridiculing people in front of others. On the other hand, he is extremely loyal to his people and very generous. In a period of three years the company has had considerable turnover and he has gone through two executive vice-presidents. They were unable to take the enormous amount of heat it took to stay in his environment. He is very intimidating. There is also a group of managers who have been with him from the beginning of the company. They know you don't listen to how he says things. You listen to what he says and only then when he isn't in the business of trying to knock you off balance. His language is extremely colorful.

I remember the first time I met him. He was a vice-president for another company. He had the reputation as a maverick even then. He was also known to be hard to hold down in one place for any period of time. I met him while doing a management development program for his company. It lasted a total of two days over a four-week period (four half-day sessions). Buck attended maybe three and a half hours of the total twelve hours. Part of the program was a follow-up meeting with each participant. You can imagine I was not looking forward to meeting with him. The first words out of his mouth were, "This training stuff is all bull . . . I hope you are getting them to pay you a lot for what you do. It's a great con." I could have responded to his tone or his words or I could do what I did. I asked him to tell me about his job and his goals. He was as clear as I have ever seen a person about his abilities and direction. He was driven to win and he judged that winning almost entirely by dollars. He would say, "No mun, no fun."

He knows instinctively most other people are far less self-reliant and directed. So, when he started his new company and began to hit some of the normal rough spots, he called me. Actually, he didn't call me directly, he had his executive vice-president call. Why? Because under all the bravado is a person truly dedicated to his goals and he knows it takes others to make that happen. He would really like to do it all himself and has no compunctions in telling you he can do your job better than you. In truth he can't do them all better but he can do many better.

When you are with him he will see the one mistake in dozens of correct items and he will confront you on that issue. He is not going to change dramatically; he doesn't trust many other people. On the other hand, if you weather the nature of the interactions and do your best, he will reward you. He has a better employee-participation profit-sharing program than any other company of similar size of which I am aware. Trying to change Buck is useless. If he perceives you as reasonably strong you can count on him to tell you the absolute, unvarnished truth. If he perceives you as weak, he will make your life miserable until you "grow up" and produce or leave. Buck is a good news/ bad news owner/CEO. The good news is you will always know exactly what he is thinking. The bad news he will tell to you in a way that, if you let it, will make you feel stupid and worthless.

Joanne is the owner and president of a consulting company. Her international client base has been built on her considerable expertise and stature in the field of management consulting. Both she and her company have the reputation for effective performance. She is a driven, clear-minded, goal-oriented leader. She is considered to be very approachable. She will listen to her employees on any matter, whether it is personal or business. As a result, her employees expect her to understand when their performance suffers. She doesn't. She sees little or no connection between listening and looking for solutions to all problems and allowing for less than each individual's personal best effort.

The underlying, and chauvinistic, expectation of the employees is that a woman will be different. When she isn't, she is viewed as not only unreasonable but also bitchy. Joanne is even-handed, fair, and demanding, traits that don't fit the fabrication others, specifically her employees, have for her as a manager. She is expected to be different; that is, gentler and softer.

She is not only misunderstood because of her ownership, presidential behavior but also because she defies the picture employees have of a woman in that role. Her female predecessors into ownership and senior management often adopted the behaviors and appearances of men. She is clear that she is a woman and sees herself as equal to all men. She doesn't use her womanhood but rather relies on her competence to accomplish her objectives.

If Joanne were a man, her behavior, though dissonant with employees' expectations, would be better tolerated. It is apparent that even-handedness when placed next to unreasonable expectations still leads to confusion. If she were a man her management style would cause employees to consider her a manager of considerable talent.

Morton is the president of a very successful health-care provider in a highly competitive urban environment. He has the reputation as a skillful, modern manager. He is the archetype of an effective CEO. He sees his job as focusing on the long term and translating that into goals and objectives for the people in the organization and then he expects others to work toward their goals. He perceives himself as being in control of both the environment and the kind of organization he directs. He feels that he leads through example. When I asked him what he meant by this he said,

> I translate our goals and objectives to them (managers) in as many ways as I can. I do that by example, by demonstrating that the planning [process] makes an awful lot of good sense, that establishing good goals and objectives, having a clear sense of the mission and then being able to translate that into an action plan, as we call it here, makes sense. I work like that. I expect them to work like that, and, obviously, while my job is to deal with the outside world, their job is to deal with the internal. I think they do their jobs better because they have a better understanding of the outside world. They feel as though they are participating more in the future of the hospital.

He sees the organization as progressive and challenging. He is clear that the organization reflects himself and his vision. Although he is open to others, he never enters significant dialogues or meetings without his own point of view clearly shaped by research and experience. There is an atmosphere of calm and control around Morton. His desk is clear. He looks directly at you when he talks to you and he smiles a lot. It is important to point out that several of the key senior managers below Morton have the earned reputation of being very authoritative in their relationship to the middle managers.

Although I had talked to Morton many times before, I wanted to get some specific responses to questions that I had in order to include them in this book. I went to the hospital late one afternoon at the appointed hour. It was at a time when there was a changing of the guard taking place. I approached the information desk where there was a frenzy of activity. I was asked by the person about to leave if she could be of service. I introduced myself and asked if she would direct me to Morton's office. When I arrived on the second floor and got lost as I frequently do, he was coming down the hall to meet me. The receptionist obviously had called to tell him I was coming. After the interview, which lasted about 45 minutes, I was going through the same lobby I had entered and was very much into my own thoughts, when over my shoulder I heard, "Mr. Blue, thank you for coming and have a pleasant day." This was coming from the person who had replaced the person I had talked to on my way in. It seemed such a good example of the nature of the environment and the commitment to quality and service.

Walt is the president and largest stockholder (not majority) of a small (about $30 million in annual sales), high-tech, defense-industry manufacturer. He is known throughout the company as a no-nonsense person. He relates well to the "people on the line." He doesn't trust any manager to do things as well as he would do them. He and several principal partners bought a company which was in Chapter 11 bankruptcy and built a financially successful, growing company.

He feels his control was greater when the company was smaller. He felt closer to the line and, consequently, the relationships were easier to handle. He realizes he has the same amount of control now but feels it is harder to exercise it. He feels he can no longer get directly to the line to solve the problem that he knows is wrong. He has to go through layers of management. He feels that the managers have a more generalized interest in problem solving and it doesn't tend to get down to the specific thing he sees. Everyone is aware of the problem but it doesn't get solved. He is frustrated.

Walt believes that the middle and senior management don't get the input from the people on the line. The managers, he believes, are relying on their own perceptions and not the views of the people who have a hands-on relationship to the problems. He believes people often avoid solving a problem for months though they know it exists. His learned management expertise tells him that he should work through the managers; his instincts tell him they can't be trusted. As a consequence, he spends a great deal of his time concerned with the day-to-day operation of the company. His managers have become accustomed to waiting for his answer, because they know he will oblige them and the answer will be (apparently) better than the one they would have come up with.

Walt is also direct and honest. If you are a manager reporting to him and you ask him a question, be prepared for an answer you can take to the bank. He is not always as forthcoming with the other owners who are in management roles because of the dynamics that surround financial participation (he definitely doesn't want to provoke dissention or disagreement), and the need for consensus on important issues of corporate direction and growth.

He is aware. Sometimes he is involved directly, sometimes he is not. His management sees him as mercurial. When he is in control of his "style," he will work it out without fanfare; when he is not, you will feel destroyed by his questions and comments, all questioning your competence. I believe his is the most common of all the top management behavior. That is, he is aware of the "right" way to go about doing what needs to be done, working through and developing middle and senior management, and he needs to win. The quality of his life and the confidence and dedication of 400 employees are at stake. When push comes to shove to meet the goals (the monthly quotas), he is an owner who pushes with a smile.

Tom is the principal owner and chairman of a large, direct-mail marketing and investment company. A strange combination you might think. Not so when the very successful direct-marketing company generates enough cash that it must be invested. Tom is a self-made success who started out with practically nothing.

Tom now manages his companies and his investments. His investments in real estate are probably in the hundreds of millions of dollars. He has no need to prove anything. He is, however, constantly striving to reach new heights—sometimes literally. He recently climbed Mount Everest.

The management people who work in his companies admire him greatly. They sometimes find his belief in the possibilities contrary to their experience of the day-to-day realities of the job. He is driven to enable everyone, on any level, to achieve their potential. He will sometimes be gone for several weeks, having left the day-to-day management of the company in the hands of a very competent president, and come back smiling broadly, saying he hopes everyone is having fun. He really means it. They think he must be out of his mind. Some of them will actually say, "If I had his money I'd be smiling too, and I'd have crazy dreams and goals too." They know, but seem to forget, that he was like that when he had no money, although he was probably less intent on everyone having fun. They also know that his clear mind and razor-sharp analytical skills enable him to see the problems in a set of figures, the hazards in a marketing plan, management deficiencies in a management team, and the way out of apparently insurmountable problems. His management team knows they can count on him when the tough decisions need to be made.

I have painted several different pictures of CEOs and owners. Some you might describe as good and others as bad. My point in describing these several modes of behavior is to contend they are all normal. What makes them normal is their relationship to the dynamics of politics, ownership, and individuals. You are probably thinking that one of them is preferential to the others. But you would have to be in the precise circumstances that they are in for that to be true. You might think you would be different. Maybe you would be and maybe the company would be more vulnerable. All the effort you can put into changing them could be saved and used to enhance productivity. We in human resources management took the decades of the 1960s, 1970s, and most of the 1980s to create nearly perfect, or semi-cloned, top managers. These people are interested in winning, guaranteeing the future, and leaving some positive evidence that they have been here. It is very hard to do that without a strong, positive ego.

The people at the top probably won't change dramatically, and that's the way it is going to be. Take their energy away. Take their ego strength away. Take their need to win away. What do you have left? You have you and me. Unless we intend to have the top job. One question you should ask yourself is whether you would take your boss's job. Not just for a day. Would you take it on with the vulnerability it brings, the politics it requires, the total absorption it demands, and the devastating implications of poor decision and choices? Would you take it on knowing it would likely break down many friendships with those people with whom you associate because you know those people are not pulling their weight?

At the top you have to work through people because they are competent, not necessarily because you like them. Below the top you have the prerogative to put relationships together because you like people. The only way people at the top pick people is on the basis of competence.

The following brief and simple exercise will help to demonstrate this point. On the lines below, write the initials of the ten to twelve people in your organization who are most significant to you in getting your job done (those above you, below you, and on your level) and the degree of friendship (from 1, for distant, to 5, for close) you have with them.

Person	Friendship	
_____	_____	☐
_____	_____	☐
_____	_____	☐
_____	_____	☐
_____	_____	☐
_____	_____	☐

_____   _____   ☐

_____   _____   ☐

_____   _____   ☐

_____   _____   ☐

_____   _____   ☐

_____   _____   ☐

Now imagine yourself in a life-threatening situation in which you know you must be able to rely completely on other people for your survival. Now go back to the list and check off in the boxes (☐) those people you would want on your team. See if all your closest friends are on the list. What do you say to those people whom you are not going to have on your team? How do you say it in a way that they understand? How do you say it in time before you fall off a cliff? Those you don't pick will say you have changed. The truth is, *you* haven't changed—the circumstances, expectations, and the needs have changed.

CEOs are extremely vulnerable. Because they delegate work, outline a direction, or articulate a vision, they are asked constantly how they want it done. They don't know. The only thing they can judge is whether it was done right and on time, which is almost always after the fact. In the day-to-day routine, CEOs are probably the weakest link. They rely almost totally on people doing what they say they will do. Almost no one gets everything done, so they rely on people to do what is right.

CEOs know they don't have any real power to do things. Though they are viewed as having infinite power, their power is more or less finite. The only thing CEOs do or make are decisions and demands. Imagine a CEO saying, "Today we are going to do, make, produce, and serve at our optimal level." That and $20 will get you your next book on "Winning Through Intimidation." Now imagine the people in the organization deciding not to produce their best. What do you have? What you have is the modern American company. Their area of greatest power is in establishing priorities. When they exercise power they determine and establish the most important elements of the environment. Everyone has power in terms of doing their jobs, but only one person ultimately has power over the direction of that doing.

What makes it happen are people who are either committed to excellence or live in fear of "not doing" their jobs. The job gets done by you and the others in the organization or it doesn't get done at all. Owners know they have no real power except in the sense of the inquisition and purge—something that occasionally happens in very small companies. That is, they assess your loyalty and dedication to their view of the world and discard you if you don't pledge unfailing faithfulness. As companies grow, that kind of conduct is replaced by more subtle forms of treatment. The visceral instincts change little; that is, the feeling that people are being disloyal, untrustworthy, or rebellious when they challenge either directly or indirectly the decisions being made. No, it isn't what happens in that still primordial thought process that changes, it is the behavior. As companies get bigger, CEOs realize everyone can't be fired. This awakened feeling of powerlessness is both a relief and a burden. A relief because the crushing weight of total responsibility, which attracted them in the first place, is replaced by a more manageable load. It is a burden because now, sometimes for the first time, it is apparent that they can only be successful through the efforts of others.

Nearly all people are overworked (Figure 2). There is often much more that needs to be done than they can do. When you ask your boss what he or she wants and the response is, "all of it," does the boss mean all of it? On one level the answer is yes; on another it is no. What the boss really wants to say is, "Why do you keep asking these dumb questions? I wouldn't ask you to do it if it weren't something that needed to be done."

On the yes level the boss is unwilling to diminish the possibilities by reducing the goals. Who knows, maybe you have a way to spin straw into gold. You don't get 80 percent by shooting for 80 percent. You probably get 80 percent by shooting for 100 per-

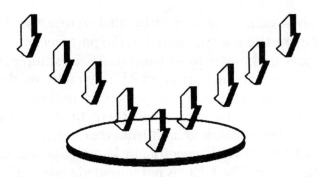

Figure 2

cent. Your challenge is to give all you can, though you will do less than all that is asked of you. Yet you will be considered a winner, because on the "no" level, the boss is completely aware that you will not get it all done. If our bosses truly meant *all*, we would *all* be fired because no one gets it *all* done. It's a game. Get it?

There is no answer to the question, "How do you expect me to get it all done?" The truth is the boss has come through the organization by only one route and knows only that path (Figure 3).

Often the person who now heads up the activity through

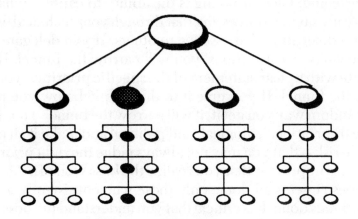

Figure 3

which the boss came to power wishes that were not so. The boss's technical expertise may be linked to the past (recent or distant) and may have nothing to do with today. As an example, the CEO may have come up from the manufacturing ranks, worked on the assembly line, from there to lead person, from there to supervising, from there to manager, from there to division director, from there to vice-president, and from there to president. However, this CEO is still only specifically knowledgeable in the area of manufacturing. The CEO is not knowledgeable in human resources, marketing, finance, research and development, or any of the other areas now reporting to the top. The further up the organization a person goes the less they know about the jobs of the people who work for them. It is best never to ask the boss any "how" questions. If you won't do it, their only viable alternative is to remove you and replace you with someone who will.

Since you can't get it all done yourself, you must be very skilled at ordering relative levels of importance on a battlefield of confusion, constant change, and sometimes misinformation. You must have well-developed skills in establishing priorities. Then, you must be proficient at delegating. Your only hope is to widen the neck of the funnel through which everything must flow (Figure 4).

The most important aptitude needed to establish priorities is clear listening. Clear listening is the ability to capture what the boss is truly saying, processing that through your technical expertise, and delegating that essence to others. If you delegate with your feelings or frustrations, you will narrow the funnel. If you delegate with a clear statement of the specific priorities, you will widen the funnel. If you give it to the people below you in the same random way you get it, it will narrow the funnel. Your job is to take the irrational, illogical, and political and make it all possible. The risk is that you may not always judge the right priorities. Again, it is important that you realize the boss won't fire anyone who doesn't get it all done, only those who consistently get the wrong things done. It is critical that you understand the boss can't really set the priorities, only establish the goal. The boss is the archer with an eye on the target. You are the bow and the people

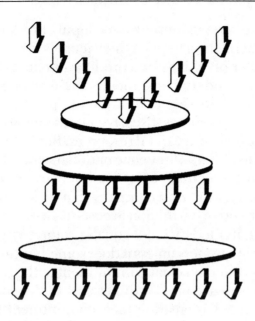

Figure 4

below you are the arrows. You must establish the right tension and direction. They will go where the boss points but only if you create the propelling energy.

The principal goal of all organizations is survival and the driving force for most CEO/owners is success. Both of these are judged in our culture by financial yardsticks. We really don't trust people who say they are successful at what they do if they haven't acquired wealth. The bank doesn't trust a company for either loans or credit lines if the company can't demonstrate a sound bottom line.

In order to be successful you must make a profit (a surplus in nonprofit organizations). In order to make a profit you must produce something. And competition is what drives us to be productive. Productivity is extremely important and almost no one has a clear understanding of it. Most people, when asked, can't even define it. How is it that something as pervasive as productivity has eluded our understanding for so long?

Productivity equals output over input. Productivity is that which we do in relation to that which it takes to do it. Productivity is the number of "things" we produce or clients that we work with or services rendered or students taught or passengers transported relative to the resources it took to produce that output. Those are human resources, fiscal resources, materials resources, property resources, and capital resources. Both input and output are measured in dollars of revenue or dollars of cost, not because of any magical power that money has but because dollars are the common denominator. So a company that makes $100 million in revenue and spends $100 million in costs has a productivity of 1.0 (that is, output divided by input equals productivity) and probably won't stay in business unless it does something about it. There is no profit there and no clear commitment to the future through research since research isn't a direct cost to the current output. Companies must demonstrate their commitment to the future through their management of productivity. To do less is to send a message of uncertainty to everyone that the company may not be there in the future.

How do you manage productivity? It is possible to increase productivity in several ways. You can maintain your output at a specific level and decrease the input (that is, reduce the expenses for materials, buildings, equipment, and people). This process has been given many names over the years, none of which has been particularly positive for the human resource. It's been called "belt tightening," "reconfiguration," and "redistribution" on the "thing" side and "layoff," "reduction in force," and, most recently, "down sizing" on the "people" side. In any event, the people who remain have more to do and less to do it with. They know that and they think it is unfair. The company can also reduce the output and reduce the input at a somewhat greater extent. The net result is the same as seen by the person.

On the positive side the company can increase its output and maintain its input at the previous level. That would work to resolve the productivity issue. But guess what, the net result to the individual is the same—more to do than resources to do it with. Probably the best solution for the long-term health of the company is to increase both output and input—only increase input slower. There it is again. The people are in the same position. So it appears that the productivity issue has a good news/bad news solution. You can find your way out but all the ways out leave the people scrambling to catch up.

Most people are not aware that it is "normal" to have too much to do and "abnormal" to get it all done. Ecopreneurs sort this out and get the right things done.

4
People

Primary Goal:
> To describe clearly the state of the work ecology now and in the foreseeable future

Intermediate Objectives:
> To describe *fair* as it relates to the world of work
>
> To explore the pictures we have of the way work should be
>
> To provide another look at the problem of having too much to do

"It just isn't fair!" I can't possibly count the times I have heard this familiar refrain. What isn't fair? There are three specific areas of contention at the center of the issue of fairness: (1) the way work gets done, (2) the way people are treated, and (3) compensation. Although Emerson may be correct that "foolish consistency is the hobgoblin of little minds," it is in the inconsistencies in these areas that the seeds of resistance are sown. There are some things that are not fair (and illegal), which we can do something about. There are other things that are simply out of line with our thoughts and we can't do anything about them. Perhaps the greatest waste of time in management is the resistance people have to the way things are. They come to work with a picture of the world as they think it should be and hold that picture up to what they find. People must develop the technology to take new, more accurate pictures. The picture they are using is generally one that they "developed" in their teens. These same people are those who are waiting for life to be without stress. Don't hold your breath.

Generally speaking, when the idea of fairness affects us in tangible ways there are things we can and should do. One of the most clear-cut, tangible issues is that of money, or salary. There is an equal pay law that guarantees no one will be paid less for substantially the same work because of age, race, color, religion, national origin, sex, handicap, or veteran status within the same organization. "Substantially the same work" applies to both the nature of the job and performance. If someone is discriminating against you in employment, transfer, promotion, compensation, training opportunity, or other measurable ways, it is not only unfair, it is illegal. If a woman is being harassed sexually, it is illegal. It is important that we differentiate between illegal and unfair.

If we are not willing to take complete responsibility for the control of our money issues, income, and financial fate, we are putting it in the hands of others who will almost certainly not meet our needs, wants, expectations, or sense of appropriateness. We live in a culture where the easiest goals to reach are financial goals. This may not be true for all Americans; it most certainly is true for the majority of people in this country. You can do a rather simple and informal study to test this assertion. Go to your local pizza shop. Pizza shops used to be owned and operated by Italians. They are now run by Greeks, Iranians, and Vietnamese.

My local shop is owned and operated by a Greek family that has been in this country for seven years. The father of the family works about 100 hours a week and the mother works about half

Figure 5

that time in the shop and the rest of the time in the home. The small children are often with her at the shop. Now, after seven years, they own the pizza shop. They also own the building the shop is in and the block the building is in. You may think they are unique. They think Americans are strange. Opportunity is everywhere and people are not taking advantage of it.

Let's try another example. I am acquainted with a woman who, in her mid-sixties, started a multilevel marketing company. You know, one of those legal pyramids that sell soaps, vitamins, clean water equipment, etc. She has been at it for the last 20 years. For the past 15 years she has been one of the top producers in the country. She makes about $20,000—only she makes that every month. So your mind is saying those pyramids count on only a few people who actually stick with it. But this is my point precisely. If you are willing to do what other people refuse to do you can make a lot of money.

Go to your local insurance company and tell them you want to sell insurance. Learn the product line, make 25 telephone calls a day to get four or five appointments to sell one policy and do that every day. You will make an impressive income and accumulate great wealth. Notice what is going on inside your head, "I don't want to sell and if I did it sure wouldn't be soap or vitamin pills or insurance." There is an axiom with regard to money that has been true since the beginning of the industrial revolution. The larger the number of people who want to do what you want to do the less you will be paid. What you need to do is what other people are unwilling to do if you want to make a lot of money, or if you want to differentiate yourself in any other positive way.

The way it works is that we want success, but we want it our way in an environment controlled by someone else who takes all the major risks. Sorry, it doesn't work that way. In a way it is always going to be unfair.

Generally, when people say unfair they are talking about the way "it makes them feel." They don't like the feeling of never quite getting the whole job done or never getting the sense that it can be done and their boss is unfriendly or mean. They don't like the feeling that whatever they do, it is never enough. These are the people who believe that life is fair when you get it all done and done right some of the time. This mental picture of fairness is the one which is taken in grade school, high school, and college. We would go to the first class and get an outline of the course, a syllabus, a reading list, and the assignments. If you do the readings, follow the syllabus, and take the tests, you get immediate recognition based on reasonably well-established standards. If you do it all and the teacher asks a question that is not directly in the materials, you can appeal and maybe even "win" a higher score or grade. I teach a course in which I require students to prepare a case study and a paper by a specific date. Everyone is to be prepared to present their case and paper at any time after that date. Some students think it is unfair. It is not truly unfair in any measurable way. It is only unfair in the way it makes them feel. They feel uncertain and not in control of the circumstances. In the real world deadlines get moved back, moved ahead, or moved around some other way. Anyone can hit a target that is nailed down. The real challenge is in hitting a moving target.

Performance evaluations are also unfair because they are often late, sometimes totally disregarded, and generally of little value or purpose. Supervisors are told they are important yet they receive little or no instruction in anything but filling out the form for the performance evaluation.

We don't like the way someone did or said something. We want the boss to be nicer or more accessible or clearer or better at two-way communications or friendlier or less direct or more discreet or less critical or more profound. In all the years of talking to people about this particular issue, I have noted one resounding fact—different people see the same person differently.

It isn't really true that they are resistant to the way things are. They are resistant to it not being the way they want it to be (Figure 6). The only way you can make it be the way you want it to be is by management of your action, reactions, attitudes, and communications (Figure 7).

Figure 6   Figure 7

Being stretched beyond what you feel are normal limits in a work world that doesn't care is the real nature of the world of work. Complaining about it sows problems in management time and the harvest it represents is lost time and continuing discontent.

EGO-CHALLENGE #1

Ecopreneurs will leave if the situation is bad enough or will take legal actions to ensure their constitutional rights; otherwise they stay and disregard the fairness or unfairness of it.

Rate yourself on the following scale:

3 — I am overwhelmed by the things that are done to me, which may not be illegal but they bug me.

to

9 — I am totally unaffected by the things that go on that cause others to complain.

| 3 | 4 | 5 | 6 | 7 | 8 | 9 |

In your words, what statement best describes your rating?

_____

_____

EGO-CHALLENGE #2

Ecopreneurs are aware that their bosses are not inclined to do effective performance evaluation, so they take the responsibility of doing their own and sit down and discuss it with their boss.

Rate yourself on the following scale:

3 — If my boss doesn't care enough to do it, I'll be damned if I will. Hell will freeze over first.

to

9 — I design my goals. I measure my progress. My boss can only measure my results. I measure myself as honestly as I can and discuss it with my boss.

| 3 | 4 | 5 | 6 | 7 | 8 | 9 |

In your words, what statement best describes your rating?

_____

_____

5
Work

Primary Goal:
To define five major attitude groups in the work world and prove each is needed to accomplish company goals

Intermediate Objectives:
To define assets and liabilities for each of the five groups

To assert that each of us is to some degree holding some of the attitudes of each group

To provide you with the opportunity to see your principal attitude about work

To give value to differing points of view about work

Work is another of those delightful four-letter words that, as a concept, is in and out of our thoughts and discussions much of the time. We normally assume others to be using similar definitions to those we are using. Nothing could be further from the truth. We can't make any assertion about people at work that applies across the board, but I think it is important for us to acknowledge that the employees we are hiring today have differing attitudes about work. Often this is more than a simple difference of opinion, it is confrontation or almost open warfare.

We have a tendency to think certain attitudes are better than other attitudes. This is actually part of a concept that you will see in refrain throughout this book. Some things are the best. We need to identify the assets in each of the various attitudinal groups we encounter and make those work for us.

Although one could categorize by age each of the attitudes and belief groups outlined below, that would be generalizing. There are people of all ages who do not share the kind of work attitude that their age group tends to have. It would also be a mistake to say it is cultural or social, since the nature of work attitudes tends to be very personal. It is more likely a function of the kind of family ecology that a person grows up in.

The first group we will discuss is the **work ethic** group; the group that's been around forever. It was there before and since the industrial revolution began. It's the group of people committed to doing a job. Their whole life is doing a job. They actually define themselves by a job. They can be counted on for getting the job done. My mother used to say, "If it is worth doing, it is worth doing well." That attitude was voiced in a somewhat more direct way by my father, who was an automobile mechanic. He used to say, "Don't do a half-assed job." It means the same thing. If it's worth doing, do it well.

Their asset is they will get the job done. If you give them a job to do, you can forget about it. It will be done. Their liability is that they are relatively insensitive to others. They don't really care what your feelings or cares are. They want the job done. It is not really fair to say they don't care about the feelings and cares of the person. It is true, however, their concern on that score is a distant second to completing the task.

They are committed to the task part of a job, and much less concerned about the people involved. It isn't that they don't care about people, or even that people are a big mystery to them. Their orientation is such that they believe that in getting the job done, people will by definition feel better about themselves, more successful, and therefore be more interested in a much fuller commitment to their life, which of course means their job. I was aware as I was growing up that my parents were not particularly interested in negotiating the appropriateness of their orientation toward getting it done, or in doing it well. That orientation didn't discount their complete love and commitment for me. The people who operate from the work ethic vantage point do so because it is the way their lives work.

There is another group of people that started entering the work culture in the 1930s and early 1940s, and whose numbers are growing. These are the **technologists**. They are scientists and engineers and all others whose focus is technical. They view work as a place where you go to solve problems because there are technical solutions. They usually don't think a problem exists unless it has a technical solution. Frequently, when working at my job in human resources in a scientific or technical environment, I would be confronted by a supervisor with this technical approach to work. The supervisor would say that there was a problem with two people who worked in the department. I would ask, "What do you want to do?" The supervisor would say, "I think I would build a wall"—a technical solution.

The technologists' asset is that they will solve every technical and scientific problem we present to them. All they need are two principal resources to solve every problem on the face of the planet. What are those two things? Time and money. They will solve water problems, air problems, nuclear problems, they'll solve them all. Their liability is that they tend to be fairly narrow in their focus and have a limited approach to problem solving.

The third group consists of recent **college graduates**. These are people with backgrounds ranging from very focused and practical to the broader liberal arts and humanities. They're coming "out" by the millions each year into the work world. They have developed a new self-image. When asked what they want to do, they will often say they don't know. When offered opportunities, they react often as though the work is somehow beneath them.

Their asset, though I'm told they can't read and write, is that they are the most broadly educated group of people in the history of any country. They know more on a broader level, and have a wider, though not deeper, education. This gives them opinions and views on many, and sometimes you might think all, things. Their liability is that they don't understand about starting at the bottom.

Another group of people are those who are affected by **civil rights** legislation. The two major constituencies are racial minorities and women. Do you think racial minorities and women are coming to work today feeling they have the same deal that white men have? Do you think women feel equal to men in access to jobs on all levels? No to both questions? Why? Because the statistics are clear. When will their attitude toward that change? When the numbers change.

Racial minorities and women in the work world today basically feel they are supposed to have an equal access but don't. Their asset, I believe, is their sensitivity to the human issues. I don't mean just women. I mean all people who have been part of a minority. They not only understand vulnerability, they see strength in it. To use a rather tired expression, "they are aware" of the human issues in the world of work. They have a sensitivity asset to offset the work ethic group's liability. I think the liability of this group is that they haven't been around enough to have all the right moves. They don't have the technology or experience. They don't have all the business skills. As I travel the country doing workshops there are always more women than men. In my opinion, the reason for this disparity in attendees is that men feel unmanageable vulnerability in demonstrating a lack of skills.

The final group is the **Me Generation**, which consists of mostly younger people. The ME stands for "my entitlement," because they feel entitled. They are the sons and daughters of people who have gone through the work world. They have parents who said, "I want you to have what I never had. I don't want you to go through what I went through. I want life to be different for you than it was for me." They have been given, and given, and given, and when they asked their parents for anything, their parents saw to it that they got the best. The kids say "I want a bike." Their parents say, "Do you want a dirt bike, a track bike, a mountain bike, a 10-speed bike, 12-speed, 18-speed, only one bike?" I remember saying to my parents, "I'd like a bike." And they said, "What a wonderful goal." Because this group's been given so much, their liability is they don't know how to earn. They don't understand about earning. They haven't had to earn.

They've also got two other major pressures on them. One, as a nationwide group this younger population can't do better than their parents. You can pick out groups in a city that can do better, but by and large they have very successful parents. My dad went through six years of education. My mother went through eight. I come from a family of 15 children. Only two of us made it through high school. When I made it through college, I was the resident guru for just having gone to school. So I've got my own business, I've got a couple of degrees, what are my kids doing? What's out there, what's the possibility for them? It isn't as easy for them to make a mark through *doing* something.

The second pressure is that they've been sitting at the dinner table every night with parents who talk about work in glowing terms such as, "How did it go today?" "It's a jungle! I hate it! I don't want to go back there! I wouldn't go back there if I didn't have to!" The kids' eyes trace the conversation from one end of the table to the other, mouths agape, and staring at their broccoli. When these kids get to be seventeen or eighteen years old and their parents say to them, "Go to work," they respond with the well-known time-out signal and say, "What, you mean that place that you've been talking about?" This generation doesn't have a very positive image about work or the work environment. And we're trying to say, "Of course, now put all that aside. It's really okay." The truth is, their parents didn't find it as bad as they portrayed it. They were only venting their frustrations. The Me Generation doesn't know that. We are going to have to do some very special things to integrate this group.

The asset this group brings to the work world looks like a liability when you first look at it. It's their absolute self-interest, which often looks like selfishness. They have been told that this country was founded on enlightened self-interest. They simply don't have the enlightenment. However, they are going to get what they want. They are the product of a society that has basically achieved its goals. You want to get a group of people connected to goals, this group understands goals. You ask them, "What do you need?" They'll have a list 20 minutes later.

Their parents put relationships together that were 50-50. Remember in the old days it was 50-50? The only problems with that is that their parents also increased their divorce rate. A lot of people got to be 50 percent, when the other 50 percent disappeared. This group understands that a good relationship is when 100 percent gets together with another 100 percent. They're going to put relationships together in totally different ways. They're going to go after what they want. They will make their mark and judge their success from the sense of self-worth and a sense of *being* and less from the process of *doing*.

Summary

We are not going to get rid of these groups. They're here to stay, to some degree. What we need to do is to weave all of these groups into one strong fabric. We need the work ethic asset of getting the job done, the ability of the technologists to solve the technical problems, the wide range of education and broad-base knowledge of the college-educated group, the willingness to deal with vulnerability and sensitivity issues of people of the civil rights group, and the awareness of the Me Generation that people are more than just the job they do.

6

Business Ecology/ Environment

Primary Goal:
To define the principal catalysts that influence the work environment

Intermediate Objectives:
To explore ownership, technology, product, geography, and human and fiscal resources

To demonstrate the stress, pressure, and force each catalyst exerts on the company ecology

CATALYSTS

All ecologies are designed to produce something. Our physical environment consists of the right proportions of elements to sustain life. As a natural ecology provides that balance for existence, a company's ecology provides the environment for productivity. In business the ownership pulls together the elements that give a company its nature. By studying the catalysts of business the way one studies natural ecology one is able to see where the company is, where it is going, and whether it's likely to get there.

Ownership

The ownership of a company is the primary influence on its own ecology. It is the first catalyst. Some might say that the business idea or the product is number one. In truth, ideas are not companies. Companies are people. It doesn't start to be a company until somebody says, "I'm going to do something with that." An idea can exist in a vacuum. A company, on the other hand, is developed through people. The ownership of companies ranges from uninvolved groups of stockholders to one person who owns a company and is ever present. However, most companies never grow to the stockholder level of ownership.

The influences of an ever-present ownership and the influences of a much larger stockholding group are vastly different. People who have a direct and immediate relationship to their company have a significant impact on that company. They are generally looking at it to determine whether or not it is fulfilling their dream—in fact, whether or not it is doing what they proposed to have done when they initially put the company together. So their perspective is that of a person who is interested in not only financial return, but also in a sense of personal worth and success. I had a conversation recently with a very successful entrepreneur about the implications of some problems in a company he owned. The entrepreneur made it clear that the company represented a small fraction of his personal wealth. Most of the other activities were in real estate and other forms of venture capital. Even though it represented such a small part of his fiscal identity, it was to a large extent his personal identity in terms of success. He was, and is, directly committed to the company's success, though its success will not have any significant impact on him financially.

Although the owners of companies are a dominant force in the day-to-day activities, they are often not well equipped to manage the day-to-day requirements of a company. They are more likely visionaries and leaders at best. Though they are involved, and have an immediate financial stake in the company, they often represent an obstacle for the people who manage the daily activities. The owners of companies can exert positive and negative pressures. They can identify direction or not identify direction. They may be clear or unclear about their expectations. They are nonetheless the significant force in the business ecology and environment. Sometimes they are a bright sun and other times they are a black hole.

ECO-CHALLENGE #1

Organizations have the opportunity to provide the clear direction and leadership that support the employees in accomplishing both the ownership's expectations and those of the employees.

Rate your organization on the following scale:
3 — We survive, succeed, or grow in spite of the ownership of this company.
to
9 — The ownership is a positive force for both organizational success and individual motivation.

3	4	5	6	7	8	9

In your words, what statement best describes your rating?

_____

_____

EGO-CHALLENGE #3

Ecopreneurs have the opportunity to use the energies in the environment, both positive and negative, as an impetus for personal excellence.

Rate yourself on the following scale:

3 — The ownership is a negative force that has a direct impact on my daily activities.

to

9 — I am able to extract from an environment elements essential for me to achieve my aims.

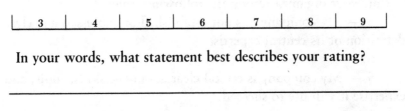

In your words, what statement best describes your rating?

_____

_____

Technology and Marketing

The second catalyst in business ecology and environmental development is the product or service. Whether a company is driven by a novel product or service, or by management or marketing expertise in search of a product or service, is significant. Scientists, through very powerful telescopes, are able to get a sense of the nature of the beginning of our universe. By being able to track it from where it was to where it is, they've been able to identify where it is going. If you look at where a company started, you should also see where it is going. This is done by looking at two things, the nature of the product or service and the corporate mission or business plan.

The nature of a company and its products or service is often not well defined inside the organization. The company's product or service or management or marketing expertise doesn't get connected to the next product or service or to the extension of the management or marketing expertise, and for this reason the organization fails. The ownership fails to draw a line from its desires and needs to the product or service that it will be producing to establish where it's going—its mission. So the nature of the process at the center of the company is an enormously important part of the organization in giving it a sense of direction. Without that sense of direction, there will be insecurity around the possibility of being or not being in business in the future.

ECO-CHALLENGE #2

Organizations have the opportunity to establish and be clear about the driving force, not necessarily the mission or goal, but the propellant or path to their goals.

Rate your organization on the following scale:
   3 — My company has not established or expressed any clear definition of its central expertise.
   to
   9 — My company is crystal clear about the skills, tools, and expertise it will use to succeed.

| 3 | 4 | 5 | 6 | 7 | 8 | 9 |

In your words, what statement best describes your rating?

_____

_____

EGO-CHALLENGE #4

Ecopreneurs understand the driving force of the company.

Rate yourself on the following scale:
   3 — I have no idea what this company thinks it's best skilled at and that makes my job nearly impossible.
   to
   9 — If I can't find it, I help create it and use it. If that doesn't work I express to the ownership (management) the assumptions I am using to accomplish the objectives for my area of responsibility.

| 3 | 4 | 5 | 6 | 7 | 8 | 9 |

In your words, what statement best describes your rating?

_____

_____

Product or Market Driven

The third catalyst is the consumer. The most typical differentiation here is whether the company is going to be driven by its product (that is, whether it's going to produce a unique product or service and then market it to the consumer), or whether it is going to be driven by its consumers (as a result respond to their changing needs). This decision is determined to a large extent by both the nature of the product and the technology surrounding it. It sounds as if it's the kind of decision most companies would make. Surprisingly, it is not a decision that most companies make.

The vast majority of companies start off being product driven. They produce a product and then sell it. Digital Equipment Corporation is a very good example. When it started in the minicomputer business it produced a product nobody else had. It made as many as it could, put them on the loading dock, and people were there waiting to take them. That continued for many years, and then slowly over time the company was asked by its consumers to configure the product in a slightly different way for their particular needs, and then the company had to start looking at whether it was going to be driven by a product that is unique and that is sold as it was, or a product that responded to the needs of the consumer. Most companies ultimately decide to respond in some way to both.

There isn't a particularly right or wrong decision here. Digital made the decision to respond to the needs of the consumer. It enabled them to continue to grow. It is entirely possible that if you were managing a company that sold bicycles and you thought you had the best possible design for a bicycle in the world, you might want to continue to produce bicycles in exactly the same way. Your market share may not grow, but that's all right. If the decision is made to be driven by the consumer, it has an important impact on the way the company is or needs to be structured. The structure of an organization must be such that it is flexible enough to respond to the next request of the consumer. Most organizations are not structured well enough to be that flexible.

ECO-CHALLENGE #3

Organizations succeed by being structured in a way that best supports their relationship to the consumer. They know if their role is to act and/or react, and structure in a way to support the decision.

Rate your organization on the following scale:

    3 — My company does not have a clear view of its relationship to the consumer, a fact that is evident in both its priorities and structure.

    to

    9 — My company is driven through its direct and clear view of its relationship to the consumer, and is structured in a way to support that relationship.

| 3 | 4 | 5 | 6 | 7 | 8 | 9 |

In your words, what statement best describes your rating?

_____

_____

EGO-CHALLENGE #5

Ecopreneurs understand the significance of the relationship of the consumer to both the everyday operation of their responsibilities and the internal interactions needed to accomplish both short- and long-term objectives.

Rate yourself on the following scale:

    3 — The relationship to the customer isn't significant to me or to the people who work for me.

    to

    9 — I use my knowledge of the relationship to the customer, which is either given to me by the ownership (management) or interpreted by me through observations, as a present and driving force in my interactions with those who work for me, my peers, and those to whom I report.

| 3 | 4 | 5 | 6 | 7 | 8 | 9 |

In your words, what statement best describes your rating?

_____

_____

Geographics and Demographics

The next major catalyst in this process is the geographical, or demographic, decision. If one were to pursue this logically, one might say that the next most appropriate catalyst would be the work force. That is, you would determine where the people are who would best enable you to provide what you want to do. In most organizations the decision about geography is made by the same person who makes the decision about what the product is going to be, what the service is going to be, whether or not the organization is going to provide something that is changing or not changing according to the consumers' needs. The location is usually in the owner's neighborhood.

The Northeast part of this country is a vastly different place from the Southwest. I know because I spend half of my time in both. I spend time with clients in Boston and I spend time writing and exploring alternatives in San Diego. Now, it's not strange that I would do work in one and develop or explore in another. The Northeast has a kind of orientation that causes you to feel it's appropriate to get focused and get involved with your work. The Southwest, on the other hand, gives you a feeling of spaciousness and openness, and the area exudes the feeling of possibilities. It is a part of the world that is open to almost anything. There are lots of people who live in the Southwest, but not very many of them are highly trained in technology or manufacturing. The obvious exceptions to these assertions are Silicon Valley and other small pockets of technology in computer manufacturing.

These geographic and demographic imperatives are significant in that they determine both the kind of attitudes about possibilities—open or closed, direct or indirect—and whether or not there is a sufficient labor pool of the type the organization needs.

ECO-CHALLENGE #4

Organizations can make valuable decisions about the geographic and demographic implications of doing business. These decisions are best arrived at by knowing the facts about the other ecological factors of ownership, product, and consumer.

Rate your organization on the following scale:

3 — My company is where it is geographically simply because of chance.

to

9 — My company's location was determined because it makes the best contribution to organizational objectives.

| 3 | 4 | 5 | 6 | 7 | 8 | 9 |

In your words, what statement best describes your rating?

_____

_____

EGO-CHALLENGE #6

Ecopreneurs use the geographical and demographical realities of the organization to help establish the true company goals. If the expressed primary goal of the organization is to produce product excellence and the company is located in a geographic or demographic environment that clearly does not support that assertion, the ecopreneur looks to determine what goal it does support.

Rate yourself on the following scale:

3 — The location of this company is of no significance to me.

to

9 — The location of this company supports me in either the accomplishment of my responsibilities or in focusing my attention on the organizational objective it does support.

| 3 | 4 | 5 | 6 | 7 | 8 | 9 |

In your words, what statement best describes your rating?

_____

_____

Work Force

The work force is the next catalyst. The nature of the work force has changed, and will continue to change. The work force as I have outlined in the preceding pages has changed in its attitudes about work. The questions here are: Is it a younger work force or an older work force? Is the work force made up of a particular ethnic group or is it made up of new arrivals to this country? The work force is the lifeblood of an organization. A company cannot produce anything without its people. Many companies seem to take a long time learning this lesson. Simply willing the company to produce its best each day without the specific intent of each of the individuals involved is wasted time.

The company's attitude toward, belief in, treatment of, and overall commitment to its work force, and its willingness to say and demonstrate through its actions what it means, to a very large extent determines the effect that work force will have on the overall business ecology. Though it is extremely important to have an ownership, a product, a technology, and a working geographic environment, without a work force that is committed to producing you have nothing. You can even have all the fiscal resources necessary to be able to succeed in ten businesses. Your work force will determine whether or not you have a positive, constructive, healthy business.

ECO-CHALLENGE #5

Organizations can be based on the understanding that all of their performance, power, and success comes from the work force. They can see that people are eager to succeed and are prepared to produce their best each day.

Rate your organization on the following scale:

3 — My company uses people like things and thinks nothing of discarding them when they are done using them.

to

9 — My company is committed to its work force. Although the company is prepared to do what must be done to survive, decisions that have a negative effect on the people are agonized over.

| 3 | 4 | 5 | 6 | 7 | 8 | 9 |

In your words, what statement best describes your rating?

_____

_____

EGO-CHALLENGE #7

Ecopreneurs know that they succeed only through the efforts of the people who work for them. They have no delusion of being able to carry the load themselves. They know their power is given to them by others and those others give it to them only out of respect.

Rate yourself on the following scale:

3 — I am in a constant tug of war with the people who work for me.

to

9 — Those who work for me are an effective, integrated team.

| 3 | 4 | 5 | 6 | 7 | 8 | 9 |

In your words, what statement best describes your rating?

_____

_____

Fiscal

The final catalyst in the business ecology is finances. Companies can be financed in many ways. Some companies are started on a shoestring. Others are started with significant venture capital. Some organizations have individuals who provide this fiscal support, and others have small groups that provide capital. It is possible for companies to succeed that are woefully undercapitalized. It is also possible for companies to fail who have considerable capitalization. In the early stages of development, you can see the behavior of a company is very much connected to the kind of finances they have. The presence or absence of money provides one basic difference from company to company: the company that has a significant amount of money has more options and can explore the possibilities of doing other things, and generally sooner. The presence or absence of money often has a more direct impact on the growth rate rather than the success of a company. Companies with little capital can be very successful. It is likely that their growth will be somewhat slower.

ECO-CHALLENGE #6

Organizations have the opportunity to be driven by fiscal concerns in a healthy way—a way which represents a positive impetus to achieve, succeed, and grow. It is also possible for companies to be obsessed by money concerns to a point where it colors not only their decisions in the early stages of development but also hampers their decision making throughout the life of the company. The impact and importance of money is a significant ingredient in all decisions. Whether it is the most significant depends on the developmental (ecological) stage of the company.

Rate your organization on the following scale:

3 — My company makes all decisions on the basis of money. It considers money first, and probably always will.

to

9 — My company places the significance of money in the decision-making process in such a way that it properly reflects its contribution and importance.

| 3 | 4 | 5 | 6 | 7 | 8 | 9 |

In your words, what statement best describes your rating?

_____

_____

EGO-CHALLENGE #8

Ecopreneurs use money considerations to determine the final direction in decision making but not in the stage of exploring possibilities and alternatives. They know that in doing so they would be limiting their perspective on the best solutions and would consistently be focusing only on the safe, well-used, and ultimately less creative solutions.

Rate yourself on the following scale:

3 — Using anything but money as the driving force in problem solving is a waste of time.

to

9 — I may settle for taking less than the best route in problem solving, but I don't stop looking at all the possibilities, because doing so would ultimately reduce both my potential and that of my company.

| 3 | 4 | 5 | 6 | 7 | 8 | 9 |

In your words, what statement best describes your rating?

_____

_____

Summary

The catalysts of the ecology of companies are the root system through which the ecology is fed. The principal tap root is the ownership. It is not only the primary source of energy, but the deepest support and stabilizing factor (Figure 8).

All the remaining catalysts are secondary to the ownership. To resist the nature of the ownership is to desire to be something other than what was represented in the seed potentiality from which the company grows.

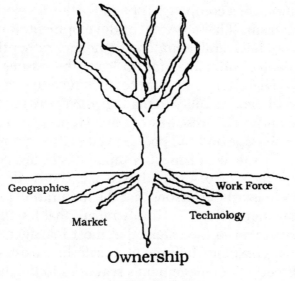

Figure 8

DEVELOPMENTAL STAGES

Primary Goal:
To define the stages through which all companies either can or do pass

Intermediate Objectives:
To identify the lessons available at each stage

To assert that lessons unlearned affect the pace, growth, and development but not necessarily survival of a company

To describe what expectations and reactions most managers have regarding learned or unlearned lessons

To assert that effective management is possible where many lessons have gone unlearned

The evolution of a company is not unlike the development of any other organism. It has a system of development. It is notable for its focus on the overall company demeanor rather than the individuals. Many companies fail to learn the lessons available at each step. Their lack of support for managers and employees can be linked to their inability to manage their way through the specific demands and pressures of each step. As a result they get stuck at one stage and the people who are the resource that determines the success of most companies get disenchanted and leave, or, even worse, lose enthusiasm and stay. Because a company fails to learn the lessons that the maturation process offers doesn't mean it will fail. It simply means that it will not support the management to the extent that most managers expect support. Most company failures or borderline existences can be linked directly to management's reactions to the unlearned lesson and to primary contributors who are pulling in different directions.

Start-Up—The Concentration Is Energy

At this stage (the *garage stage*—so called because of the large number of companies that begin out of someone's garage or basement) almost everything is focused on survival needs (equipment, materials, customers, and space). Everyone and everything pulls together. Conservation of all resources is critical. The one area where this is not necessarily true is in the area of personal time. There is little thought about whether there is the precise balance of power, skills, or vision of the future. The basic driving force is to not fail. Every resource is stretched to its capacity—the human resource, the material resources, the buildings and other physical resources, and particularly the fiscal resources. These are the days which in the future will be called the "good old days." I have watched many companies go through this stage. It is exciting and all-consuming. It is, at once, incredibly powerful and exciting because the focus and attention is on the present, and scary because it could all be for nothing. In terms of tangible resource management, it is the best managed in all the phases of company development.

ECO-CHALLENGE #7

Organizations can learn the lessons of resource and energy conservation available at this stage.

Rate your organization on the following scale:

3 — Though no longer in the start-up stage, my company's focus is on failure and very short-range objectives—success is measured on daily, weekly, or monthly goals.

to

9 — My organization knows the value of conservation of resources and looks longer term for its sense of success and direction.

| 3 | 4 | 5 | 6 | 7 | 8 | 9 |

In your words, what statement best describes your rating?

_____

_____

EGO-CHALLENGE #9

Ecopreneurs are aware their resource conservation is essential in order to meet the challenge of the job.

Rate yourself on the following scale:

3 — I am overwhelmed by the things that are done to me and have little control over resources.

to

9 — I am unaffected by the things that go on and I maintain a keen perspective on resource management.

| 3 | 4 | 5 | 6 | 7 | 8 | 9 |

In your words, what statement best describes your rating?

_____

_____

Foothold—The Concentration Is Expertise

The basic needs of the company are now being achieved—the payroll is being met, the product or service works, and consumers are showing a serious interest. Now the issues shift to whether it can continue to grow and provide longer-term security. The problems confronted now are security and maintenance. It is a time to put up a line of defense to protect the company from anything that could threaten its existence. The primary focus here is productivity. Almost all the meetings and reports are to determine the integrity of deadlines. The thought process shifts from survival to preservation of the accumulated resources. A subtle shift I will grant you, but a significant one nonetheless. It is here that the early signs of reduced risk-taking can be seen.

ECO-CHALLENGE #8

Organizations can learn the lesson of productivity definition and measurement.

Rate your organization on the following scale:

3 — My organization has no clear perception of productivity definition or measurement.

to

9 — My organization has a clear perception of productivity definition and measurement.

3	4	5	6	7	8	9

In your words, what statement best describes your rating?

_____

_____

EGO-CHALLENGE #10

Ecopreneurs are aware they must be clear about productivity and express their views to the people who work for them in order to meet the challenge of the job.

Rate yourself on the following scale:
3 — I am unclear about productivity and consequently those who report to me do not know how I will react from day to day.
to
9 — Those who report to me are fully aware of my definition of productivity and my personal commitment to it.

| 3 | 4 | 5 | 6 | 7 | 8 | 9 |

In your words, what statement best describes your rating?

_____

_____

Niche—The Concentration Is Emotion

The questions now shift to the company's relationship to the competition, its corporate mission, and product prominence. This is definitely a period of good news/bad news. The good news is the future of the company is more than a mere possibility; it is a near certainty. The bad news is the company now must take responsibility for planning the future and attaining growth to its corporate potential. For the first time, the future becomes a regular part of everyday discussions. All of the energies that came from the desire to win, or more accurately not to fail, no longer have the same impact. It is not the same to be pushed from failure as to be drawn toward goals or the corporate mission. The mission and the company goals need to be developed with the kind of clarity that enables people to align with it.

At this stage everyone has a chance to look up from their work benches or desks and assess the company's commitment to these broader issues, not only in its relationship to the broader issues of mission and the future but also the relationship of the major contributors. It is here that two major problems often surface. The major individual contributors are often not clear what their needs are or how to express them, which means the mission of the company can get garbled or amorphous if it tries to include needs of all the significant players. Simple little words such as *a* or *the* can have an enormous impact on the mission statement. It doesn't make any difference whether the mission is written or not. Everyone in the organization has a constant internal dialogue about the company. One person may be thinking that "JenCorp is *a* leader . . ." and another may be thinking, "JenCorp is *the* leader. . . ." There's a big difference between *a* and *the*. Also one principle could be thinking the company will be a leader in technological *innovation* and another could be thinking the company will be a leader in technological *applications*. In the first instance there would need to be a significant financial commitment to research and development to assure primacy in the field. In the second instance there would need to be more commitment to market needs and the applications required to maintain primacy in the field.

As I have said several times, the mission of a company is incredibly important. It is important in the sense that it gives people a feeling, or an understanding, that the company is committed to its future. Without a clear statement of its mission, a company is leaving the question about the future unanswered.

ECO-CHALLENGE #9

Organizations can understand the importance of a defined mission and the significance of a game plan to attain it.

Rate your organization on the following scale:
3 — My organization has no mutually agreed-to mission. Consequently the game plans are as diverse as the number of people with power.
to
9 — My organization is establishing/has established the company mission and a clear game plan to attain it.

| 3 | 4 | 5 | 6 | 7 | 8 | 9 |

In your words, what statement best describes your rating?

_____

_____

EGO-CHALLENGE #11

Ecopreneurs are clear about both their personal mission and the corporate mission and can and will talk to anyone at any time with great clarity about both. They go out of their way to find the corporate mission, even if it is muddled in the ownership, by listening to the leadership and watching the company's actions as it confronts conflicts and pressures.

Rate yourself on the following scale:

3 — I am unclear about the corporate mission and I am at a loss to explain it to the people who work for me.

to

9 — I am completely confident that I have both a philosophical and working understanding of the company mission and I have shared it with those who report to me.

| 3 | 4 | 5 | 6 | 7 | 8 | 9 |

In your words, what statement best describes your rating?

_____

_____

Image—The Concentration Is Ego

More widespread name recognition and problems of abundance mark this stage. Not for the first time but most certainly in the most direct way the egos of the key people become predominant. The company has established its expertise and is making money, sometimes a lot of money. Often the principals have become more prominent in their communities, churches, professional organizations, etc. They are clear that they are more than their jobs. Where in the early stages they were consumed by their jobs, the job is a means to something else now. It is a stage of enormous pain for most people and that pain is seen both at home and on the job.

There is nothing quite like a person who is ready to be propelled into their destiny and doesn't have a focus or direction. Many, if not most, of their dreams have been realized. In reaction to their uncertainty they will either manifest a new set of objectives or they will begin to act in apparently self-destructive ways. They will want to take unnecessary risks at work in order to stay on the edge of disaster so that they can draw the energy and adrenaline from the stress that is created. Some will become greatly depressed, and out of that depression may emerge a dogmatic, cynical, and phlegmatic person.

On a company level the questions now concern expansion, diversification, and profit. Do we stay small or do we grow? Do we add to our product line or services? Is there any more profit available from increasing in size? If the ownership is diverse, it is here that significant differences will emerge. The conservatives will want to stay small and control and protect. The radicals will want to grow, simply "because it is there," and gamble and be more vulnerable. If the ownership is in the hands of one person, the company will take the direction the owner feels most comfortable with. They will listen to both general business and financial advisers and then pretty much do what they intended to do anyway.

It is almost a certainty that there will be major differences here, because the needs of the company are really the collective needs of all the principal players. Unfortunately, each person does not stay in sync with every other person as the company evolves. This is a stage when the company can easily factionalize. It doesn't mean the company will go out of business. It does mean that most of its accomplishments will occur only with great pain and agony and often in spite of the behavior of the key players or ownership. It won't be anything like the image they had in their heads when they started, but it will be financially solvent.

ECO-CHALLENGE #10

Organizations can develop a corporate perspective of the future and have an effective forecasting technology.

    Rate your organization on the following scale:

        3 — My organization has no clear focus on the future and no effective technology to forecast it.

    to

        9 — My organization has a clear focus on the future and an effective technology to forecast it.

| 3 | 4 | 5 | 6 | 7 | 8 | 9 |

In your words, what statement best describes your rating?

_____

_____

EGO-CHALLENGE #12

Ecopreneurs are aware of the past and present circumstances of the company and can provide a clear projection of the future.

    Rate yourself on the following scale:

        3 — I am not aware of anything but the current conditions of the company and sometimes I am not even sure about that.

    to

        9 — I am totally clear about the future direction and success of the company as a result of specific knowledge I have gathered about the past and present conditions and I share that direction with those who work for me.

| 3 | 4 | 5 | 6 | 7 | 8 | 9 |

In your words, what statement best describes your rating?

_____

_____

Potential—The Concentration Is Exposure

During this phase the company is exposed to the possibilities and potential of a fully actualized organization. This phase represents the unification of all the major needs of the principal players under a mission broad enough to meet the needs of everyone. Many of the people who started the company are ready to move on to the next challenge, or should be. They don't move on in anger. They have received all that is available in the company to meet their needs. They are not long-term managers; they are people who start things so they can go on to their next challenge.

This rarefied space, into which very few companies actually get, is attained through individual expression of serious needs and the willingness to listen. Through choice the company arrives at a point that gives credence to everyone and protects everyone's needs. Sounds impossible, doesn't it? That's why I said it is the extraordinary company or organization that succeeds at this level. It happens through choice and not control.

Most of the issues now concern the future of the company—the product and its people. The mission or goals are expressed clearly and understood by *all* the people in the company. The company is committed to the mission because it is a natural and logical direction. The future of the product is inarguable because the company is committed to planning. The people are committed to the mission because it has a clear and direct bearing on their own goals. The exposure is not to risk and uncertainty, but rather to the light of day. The company can withstand scrutiny. The people in the company are proud and express that pride openly. Now the questions turn to future ownership.

New management is needed at this stage. Many of the people who started the company are entrepreneurs. They operate out of the absolute sense to win. They have a perfectionist sense of the challenge in front of them, and they are highly competitive. These people need to move on to their next challenge, and allow room for more traditional management to take over the company and its growth. Unfortunately, this step often takes place with great reluctance. The people who start the company are unwilling to give up either their philosophical control or their specific control of the company. Once control is relinquished, over time the ownership will be transferred to the public, and from the public to the board of directors. The board of directors eventually will ask these people to leave.

ECO-CHALLENGE #11

Organizations can learn to listen to the needs of the people in the organization and those of the client or consumer. Their mission is expressed in both actions and words, and people exhibit considerable pride in the company.

Rate your organization on the following scale:
3 — My organization must be stuck somewhere else, it sure doesn't fit the description above.
to
9 — People get up in the morning and are eager to come to work; this is true of both long-timers and newly hired people.

| 3 | 4 | 5 | 6 | 7 | 8 | 9 |

In your words, what statement best describes your rating?

_____

_____

EGO-CHALLENGE #13

Ecopreneurs are aware of the contribution of mission, goals, objectives, planning, and communication.

Rate yourself on the following scale:
3 — I have no time to do anything except what is on my plate at any given time and the people who work for me know that.
to
9 — I tie my goals and objectives for my area directly into corporate goals and objectives. The people who work for me know how and what they do affects the corporate performance.

| 3 | 4 | 5 | 6 | 7 | 8 | 9 |

In your words, what statement best describes your rating?

_____

_____

Summary

Companies, much like people, can be tracked through stages of development (Figure 9). The principal stages of energy (start-up) and expertise (foothold) lead to the more esoteric and dramatic stages of emotions (niche) and egos (image) and ultimately to the stage of exposure (potential).

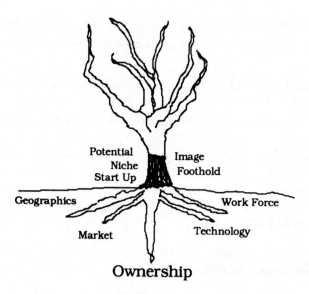

Figure 9

Companies that do not or cannot work out the challenges inherent in each stage will either fail or drop back to an earlier stage where survival is possible. Most companies struggle at the level above the one at which it finally settles, and in doing so, take up the problems and issues associated with that stage. Again, this is not good or bad, it is simply the way it is. What is good or bad is the way managers relate to the reality.

MANAGEMENT STAGES

Primary Goal:
To examine the developmental process of management

Intermediate Objectives:
To introduce the concept of management conflict

To demonstrate the relationships and characteristics of each step

To acknowledge the facts of the stunting of the development of management in most companies

To examine the opportunity to experience how you allow your company's management nature to affect you

In the last section on developmental stages, we focused on the dynamics of the organization as an entity. Although individuals were discussed to some extent, the goal was to look at the evolutionary stages of an organization. In this section on management, the goal is to examine the developmental process of the management. It is important to understand that successful group process leads to an integrated work group or team through a series of clear, well-defined steps.

Group Process

The first stage is the introductory stage, where one gets to know others. At some point roles begin to be either taken or given to people. As people begin to operate out of those roles, conflict arises. The real question isn't whether or not organizations will have conflict. The question is whether or not the organization will learn to exercise management conflict. To be able to express a conflict is not the same as to experience management conflict. So some organizations don't get through the stage of learning how to manage conflicts, and for this reason never have an integrated group or team. Teams are integrated through the management of the kinds of issues that come up as people define their roles; that is, through management conflict.

This is also true in families. Fully integrated families have learned to have family conflict. When children become teenagers, it is not a question of whether or not there will be conflict. The question is whether or not the parents will be able to handle family conflict effectively. Handling conflict effectively relies on the ability to take action, to represent yourself fully and with integrity, rather than taking a posture of reacting to situations as they occur. In the family, it is clear that people want limits that are defined and clearly stated. The same thing is true in the work world. Management conflict is managed effectively by expressing clearly the expectations, or standards, for people in their work and holding people to them.

Creation—Introduction

This is a stage of great energy and risk-taking. The emotion of the day is excitement and the hormone is adrenaline. This stage is characterized by long hours and in recollection becomes the "good old days." People are in love with life and each other. Those people who are only casually acquainted will work together as though they were lifelong friends. This happens because everyone shares a common goal—the inception (birth) of a new entity in a space previously occupied by a vacuum. Roles are unclear at this stage and as a consequence the resource that is squandered most is time. There is a greater chance that things will be done redundantly than that things will fall through the cracks.

At this stage of the development of a company the people in it are defined by it. That is, their identity is almost totally their job.

Personal relationships are secondary to the job, including marriages. The partners in the relationship often agree, either openly or by mutual acknowledgment, to a deal in which the future will have the payoff for the lack of time, attention, and companionship in the present. Positive attitudes abound in the creation stage.

One thought keeps coming to mind as I look at companies that have been successful in passing through the early stages of development: There is a much clearer association with the positive attitudes that the people have who started the organization than there is to the level of skill or intelligence.

As the company grows its disposition about positive attitudes in our corporate environments changes. People with fairly constant positive attitudes and intentions are thought to either be "on" something or lying. Yet all the studies of highly successful people demonstrate there are only a few clearly relevant characteristics common to all, or nearly all, very successful people. Native intelligence plays a part as does education, but on balance attitude is at least five times more important. It isn't necessary to do a costly research program to determine the truth in this statement. If you think of the people you know who are very successful, you will note they are positive people.

The unique thing about the creation stage is in the fact that nearly everyone is positive in their approach. They look at the negative possibilities only long enough to create both attitudinal and practical interventions. Failures at this stage often happen because people are unwilling to make the personal investment of time and energy required to meet the challenges or maintain the positive attitudes.

The principal issues are success and failure. These issues are very personal. Since a person who would start such an enterprise is both focused and highly motivated, the question of success is both personal and corporate. There is no virtue at this point in the development of the company to look to what others are not capable of doing. The important issues are what the person can add to the mixture and adrenaline is almost all some people bring. I am constantly amazed to see what it takes to be successful early on as a company emerges from either the ashes of Chapter 11 or where nothing existed before. When I was a young man I thought it was certainly daring, skill, and competence that made people and companies successful. To be successful in the early stage takes grit, a positive attitude, and a lot of hard work.

ECO-CHALLENGE #12

Organizations can learn the lessons of individual behavior and attitude.

Rate your organization on the following scale:

3 — Though no longer in the creation stage, my company's focus is on failure and very short-range objectives. People seldom leave work with a feeling of success.

to

9 — My organization is learning (or has learned) the value of conserving resources (including human resources), positive attitudes, and looking to the long term for its sense of success and direction. People get recognition for their contribution in terms of both results and effort.

| 3 | 4 | 5 | 6 | 7 | 8 | 9 |

In your words, what statement best describes your rating?

_____

_____

EGO-CHALLENGE #14

Ecopreneurs are aware their attitude must be positive in order to meet the challenge of the job.

Rate yourself on the following scale:

3 — I am overwhelmed by the things that are done to me and have little control over my attitude.

to

9 — I am totally unaffected by the things that go on and I maintain a positive attitude.

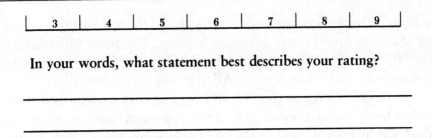

In your words, what statement best describes your rating?

_____

_____

Structure—Role Definition

Early on, the roles are muddled with considerable overlap and gaps. When leadership begins to emerge, however, the company begins to take on more formal attributes. The principals look to one another and start to make conscious divisions of responsibilities. Someone is given the responsibility of keeping a lid on the financial demands, both inside and outside the company. The person with the best skills in finance from the "group" takes over the principal responsibility for this. The nature of this responsibility can range from direct, hands-on control to interfacing with the person or company providing this service. In any event, it is important to note this person gets the job not because he or she is the best person from the general population but because that person is from the start-up group. The same process is true for the other major functions of general management, production, sales, etc.

Company goals are still rather short term in nature. People now look to each other for specific support and expertise. They are thinking, "Where are the dollar drains of the company and is everyone pulling their own weight?" Everything is still focused on the company. It is here that the seeds of disagreement are sown. The knowledge that has always been there now begins to make a difference. Not everyone is making the same level of contribution to the success of the company, though everyone may be making the same level of commitment. Differences in degree of competence are becoming clearer daily.

At this stage (foothold) the company will make its first conscious decision to "stash" someone—to get someone out of the mainstream so they won't get in the way. This person is someone who is not fully competent, yet has been there from the beginning and is owed something for loyalty. The most unfortunate part in this is that everyone involved is aware, often including the person, of what is happening. All of the key players will tell you it is the "right" thing to do. Why? Because that person was there when he or she was needed and the company must be there for that person now. Chances are you know someone in your organization who has been "stashed." Ecopreneurs do not come in with a wide broom and sweep all these people out the door. Many of them are now "corporate creations" and have no place to go. On the other hand, ecopreneurs don't make any new ones.

Throughout this stage organizations allocate responsibilities to people who have the skill to carry them out. At the same time organizations must be direct with the people who are not right for the future of the company, and assist them in looking for options and alternatives outside the company.

ECO-CHALLENGE #13

Organizations have the opportunity to confront the inevitable shortcomings of the major participants to meet the expanding and changing needs of the company.

Rate your organization on the following scale:

3 — My organization has allocated roles, and most of the important roles are filled with people who are only marginally competent and who would not rate as finalists in an open recruitment program.

to

9 — My organization is in, or has emerged from, the structure (role definition) stage and most of the important roles are filled with people who are fully competent.

| 3 | 4 | 5 | 6 | 7 | 8 | 9 |

In your words, what statement best describes your rating?

_____

_____

EGO-CHALLENGE #15

Ecopreneurs are aware they must be clear about personal success and failure with the people who work for them in order to meet the challenge of the job.

Rate yourself on the following scale:

3 — I avoid taking any direct actions with people who are not meeting the requirements of their jobs.

to

9 — I am at ease in dealing with both success and failure with the people who report to me because I know I can make it a positive experience for them.

| 3 | 4 | 5 | 6 | 7 | 8 | 9 |

In your words, what statement best describes your rating?

_____

_____

Actions and Reactions

The question isn't whether there will be conflict, but over which issues the conflict will be, and can the company evolve fast enough to focus management conflict technologies on business issues and not on petty, reactive problems. This is a very important stage in the development of the company and all points of view must be heard, yet frequently are not. Schisms are quite common during this period. The person providing the general management will have one point of view and the person responsible for production will have another. Generally, the player with the most power will take control of both the direction of the company and the day-to-day steps required to get there. This power can come from ownership, or the majority share, or it can come from affiliation with or the confidence of the ownership of the company. There is a good chance that the company will begin to take on a direction and shape that is different from what some of the early formulators would like it to be.

This is a period of particularly difficult personal decisions. The company looks as if it will not only make it but could make it "big." As a manager do I stay and align myself to a mission that I don't fully agree with and therefore subjugate my personal needs and ego, or do I leave and perhaps miss out on a once-in-a-lifetime opportunity? This is a decision to be made consciously and clearly. Otherwise what happens is what happens altogether too often. People don't express their positions and fail to make conscious decisions. It weighs on them and becomes a source for their criticism in the future whenever there is an opportunity to say "I told you so." And there are always going to be opportunities to say that even in the best of companies. Everyone in a key management role must either buy a ticket on the express or get off the train.

Ecopreneurs will step to the side, not back, in order to take stock of the situation. They reassess their needs and precisely what it is they get from their roles. How are their needs nourished from their jobs and how are they not? How do their needs align with other significant participants in their lives—spouse, children, etc.? Ecopreneurs are careful to negotiate from their own needs and they make conscious decisions to modify their direction from a position of control and choice. But that after all is the basis for all relationships.

ECO-CHALLENGE #14

Organizations can develop a corporate and individual approach to conflict.

Rate your organization on the following scale:
    3 — My organization avoids conflict and when it is addressed it is with a heavy hand.
    to
    9 — My organization encourages people to not only express problems but also look for a win-win outcome.

| 3 | 4 | 5 | 6 | 7 | 8 | 9 |

In your words, what statement best describes your rating?

_____

_____

EGO-CHALLENGE #16

Ecopreneurs are aware that to manage is to create conflict. They are aware of the conflict created. They acknowledge it and discuss its implications with the people who report to them. They recognize that it is in expressing the truth that most management conflict is created and because of that it can be a positive force to accomplish objectives.

Rate yourself on the following scale:
3 — My instinct is to avoid all possible conflict.
to
9 — I use conflict as a barometer to measure the degree to which I am consistently telling the truth to those who work for me.

| 3 | 4 | 5 | 6 | 7 | 8 | 9 |

In your words, what statement best describes your rating?

_____

_____

Integrated Management

This is the stage at which companies should have integrated management teams. It is a stage where problem solving should draw on the best thoughts of the people without regard to their level of prominence in the company. The exact opposite is what we find in most companies. People go to the meetings because they are on a certain level and not necessarily because they can make a contribution to the problem at hand. People are listened to because they have a bigger job, desk, and office, not because they have an appropriate contribution to make. An integrated team knows the group is more than the sum of its parts. It doesn't matter whether the exercise is a fantasy challenge on the moon or in a jungle or whether it is a real organization problem; the team results are better. In integrated management the assets and liabilities of all the players are known and discussed.

ECO-CHALLENGE #15

Organizations can learn the value of putting teams together on the basis of skills, needs, and commitment in resolving the problems.

Rate your organization on the following scale:
    3 — My company meetings are too numerous, too long, and totally unproductive.
      to
    9 — My company puts teams together by establishing where the resources are that will act on the problems and using those resources.

3	4	5	6	7	8	9

In your words, what statement best describes your rating?

_____

_____

EGO-CHALLENGE #17

Ecopreneurs in teams make a contribution to solving problems and listen to others for better and often more innovative ideas. They make the assumption they are not expert at everything and are willing to say so.

Rate yourself on the following scale:
    3 — I haven't got the time to listen to everyone, particularly when I know I am right.
      to
    9 — I am aware being right all the time doesn't leave any room for creativity and growth in others.

| 3 | 4 | 5 | 6 | 7 | 8 | 9 |

In your words, what statement best describes your rating?

_____

_____

Summary

Although it is possible to evolve positively and naturally through the management process to integrated groups and teams, it is more likely companies will get "stuck" at one of the intermediate steps (Figure 10). The most common stalling point is at the structure (role definition) stage. In order to have a fully integrated management the company must learn effective management conflict technologies. Since most don't, they settle into the last fully experienced step, which is role definition. Consequently, the company becomes a place where things get done because "I am the boss."

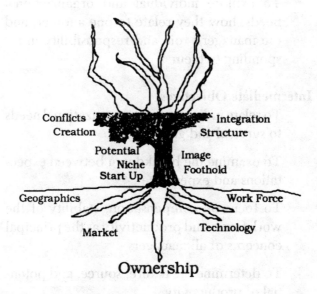

Figure 10

7

Individual and Organizational Needs

Primary Goal:
To explore individual and organizational needs, how they relate to one another, and the manager's role and responsibility in responding to them

Intermediate Objectives:
To relate individual and organizational needs to survival and growth

To examine the breakdown between expectations and experience

To focus on compensation, stability of the work force, and productivity as the principal concerns of all managers

To determine the nature, source, and potential of productivity

All entities exist within a hierarchy of needs. Fortunately, we had Abraham Maslow, who understood that hierarchy well enough to describe it to us many years ago. Although he described it in terms of individual needs, it is my observation that this hierarchy also exists in social entities, in all forms of groups and processes such as the family and the work world. Maslow observed there are different levels of needs and that as we satisfy needs on one level, we tend to move to the next level. He also noted that satisfaction of the previous level did not need to be complete. It only needed to be satisfied to a level where we would become open to the possibilities available to us on other levels of needs. He described a lower order of needs and a higher order of needs. There is something to be learned from each need in the hierarchy of needs. On the first level of needs, the physiological, we can satisfy not only our need for air, water, food, sex, etc., but also learn the qualitative lessons relating to good and bad air, water, food, sex, etc. For many people, most of the satisfaction on the lower levels, safety, physiological, health, and security/economic needs, comes in the form of quantity. The higher order of need, relationships, ego and recognition, and self-actualization, are almost totally grounded in quality.

Many people and many companies move through the several levels of needs without experiencing or learning the quality possibilities. They will experience growth, the quantity factor in the actualization of the organization, but will not experience potential, the qualitative factor in the actualization of the organization. Growth combined with potential links bigger with best and the best is contributed by the people. Many companies never learn that the shortest route to maximized productivity and growth is maximized individual potential. Some people, some organizations, and some social entities don't seem to grow at all. They are pleased with where they are, they like the order of things, the predictability, and the comfort.

People come to work without personal goals. A bold statement, I admit, but I assure you it is true. If you doubt it is true, start with yourself, and then ask a few people if they feel pleased with the clarity with which they look to the future. Goals are needed now because the world has changed. We are no longer simply satisfying basic needs. Our parents had to put food on the table, clothes on our backs, and roofs over our heads. Today people are looking to satisfy more sophisticated needs. This requires that we be clear about our goals. It doesn't necessarily mean we have to write them down, but it is critical that we identify them. The majority of people come to work without a sense of where they're going, assuming that their organization, at the very least, knows where it's going. And frequently they find it isn't so.

The next thing people expect as they come to work is that they're going to be managed by people who are skilled at supervision. This would be extraordinarily funny if it weren't so painful. Most of us get to be supervisors by magic. One day we're not, the next day we are, and our organizations don't bother to train us. They don't even take the time to go through a policy manual, if there is one, and explain the policies, precedents, or circumstances under which it might be used differently. Nor do they explain that a policy is a guideline. These supervisors aren't skilled at management. The expectation people have isn't met at the very basic need level.

The organization, beyond its need for a mission, is looking to have people working for it who are motivated; that is, motivated and committed to doing an effective job. Supervisors are often told they have the responsibility to motivate their employees. This is probably one of the most direct reasons why people feel they are failures in the job of supervising.

Motivation isn't something that happens from outside a person. The most we can expect from the skilled supervisor is to create an environment within which motivated people will develop. It is unfair and counterproductive to put the responsibility of motivating people on a supervisor who has no real control to begin with. The way to motivate people is to manage their needs in the workplace, which we must do in an organization with needs that also must be managed.

The following material is presented not for you to be concerned that your company did or didn't learn the lesson, but to recognize what lessons are available at each level of managerial needs and how you may or may not be acting and reacting because your company did or didn't learn the lesson.

JOB AND FAIR PAY/STABLE AND TRAINED WORK FORCE

People—Job and Fair Pay

The basic need people have at work is a clearly defined job and fair wages. What makes compensation fair is that people understand it to be equitable within the company. Fair compensation means that one's pay is consistent with what others with similar backgrounds and similar responsibilities are paid. If an employer cannot explain the way in which salaries are determined, the employer is not meeting the most basic employee needs. Employees may not be motivated by money but they most certainly are demotivated by either perceived or real unfair compensation. The basis for compensation should be discussed before a person comes to a job. The most common contributing factor for the initial phases of discontent is that there is no rationale for the compensation people receive. External equity, the relationship of compensation to your competition, does not ultimately decide one's pay. That's a philosophical and financial decision of the organization. I know many companies that pay somewhat less than their competition and have content, motivated employees. I know of no company with internal equity problems that has content, motivated employees. Often companies will attempt to keep compensation information out of the hands of the employees. Two things happen as a result: (1) people talk to one another anyhow, and (2) they assume the company has something to hide.

Company—Stable and Trained Work Force

The first level of need an employer has is stability. The organization's basic need is a stable and trained work force—not total stability, however. A totally stable work force would lead to stagnation. An acceptable level of turnover is essential. Our work force has become very mobile. The work world is experiencing incredible turnover. The turnover rate in many industries averages 20-25 percent a year. I have a client who was experiencing turnover at such a rate that people just appeared to be going in the front door and out the back door. They hired over 170 people one year, and in that same year they lost nearly 120 people.

It's easier to recruit people than it is to keep them. Most supervisors understand that. Most supervisors also don't know what they have to do in order to keep people. Again, part of what you do to keep people is to meet the needs of the individual. The lack of stability means supervisors spend a lot of their time recruiting and training. Their time gets drained off doing the training that they wouldn't otherwise have to do if they weren't constantly being confronted by new people.

Because turnover is often higher than expected, most people at work are only partially trained. Being only partially trained is a natural condition of work. We are all generally "works in process." However, the degree to which the average person is trained is much lower today than it was 20 years ago. Some people are fully skilled in their jobs while most are in the process of learning.

ECO-CHALLENGE #16

Organizations have the opportunity to learn the significance of providing fair wages and communicating their commitment to the work force in terms of internal salary equity.

Rate your organization on the following scale:

3 — There is considerable distress between the company and the employees regarding compensation but very little of it is on the surface.

to

9 — People understand the rationale for their compensation and feel comfortable in asking questions or expressing concern if they perceive a problem.

| 3 | 4 | 5 | 6 | 7 | 8 | 9 |

In your words, what statement best describes your rating?

_____

_____

EGO-CHALLENGE #18

Ecopreneurs know the relationship between the organizational philosophy and individual compensation, and can explain it to their staff.

Rate yourself on the following scale:

3 — Compensation is beyond my control and I don't understand how it works in any event.

to

9 — People who work for me have already been told the relationship between the organization's compensation philosophy and system and know they can count on me to fight to see that their pay reflects honestly the contribution they make to the company.

| 3 | 4 | 5 | 6 | 7 | 8 | 9 |

In your words, what statement best describes your rating?

_____

_____

ECO-CHALLENGE #17

Organizations that are most successful know the importance of a stable and trained work force and the relationship between that stability and the level of proficiency or level of training of the work force. They are committed to having not only the right level of turnover but also in not losing their best talent.

Rate your organization on the following scale:

3 — My company's turnover is neither controlled nor understood.

to

9 — My company has not only let every supervisor know that managing turnover is a significant part of their job but has given the supervisors support in accomplishing that goal.

| 3 | 4 | 5 | 6 | 7 | 8 | 9 |

In your words, what statement best describes your rating?

_____

_____

EGO-CHALLENGE #19

Ecopreneurs don't accept concepts like the industry average to determine the acceptability of any level of turnover. They are aware that losing the talent important to the goals of the company needs to be examined regardless of how low the overall turnover rate is.

Rate yourself on the following scale:
  3 — I have no control over turnover.
  to
  9 — I know that when someone leaves the company voluntarily from any area for which I am responsible it is because they are going to a better opportunity and not because they feel compelled to leave.

| 3 | 4 | 5 | 6 | 7 | 8 | 9 |

In your words, what statement best describes your rating?

_____

_____

PERFORMANCE STANDARDS/ MAXIMUM PRODUCTIVITY

People—Performance Standards

The second level of need that individuals have is to know the standards of performance against which they are going to be judged. Most people learn the standards over time and as they fail to meet them. We don't explain standards of performance. Often the scenario goes something like this: "Blue, I want to see you in my office at one o'clock and I'm sure you know why." Now I get an hour or two to try to figure out what I have done wrong. There's an underlying belief I did something wrong. I'm not quite sure what it was, but I'm about to find out. Why is it people don't know what the standards are in their jobs? Is it because supervisors don't know that it's important to tell people what the standards are? Or, is it because we don't know how to express standards? We haven't figured out a way to deal with all or most of the complexities of today's work setting.

Standards aren't easily defined by most people in management. When I ask supervisors what their performance standards are, I get blank stares. I don't understand why that is so. The concept of standards is something that is ingrained in our everyday work world. And yet we don't know how to define it. People will say, "Well, it's got something to do with measuring, it's got something to do with quality, it's got something to do with quantity." And then in the process of pursuing the question, people will begin to say, "It seems to me it's something against which you measure something else. It's a kind of yardstick." Standards are yardsticks. Standards are references. They are reference points against which you measure something.

Since the early 1900s, and more specifically since World War II, time and motion studies have established what the average person should be able to do in various work environments. What we have done with these standards is point people in their performance toward an average. Now that we've managed to achieve average as actual performance, we're not happy. The way we deal with the need for better performance is through incentives, which are a premium for better than average performance.

Nearly all the definitions used in current dictionaries equate standard to this concept of averageness. They will use definitions such as, "an accepted measure of comparison for quantitative and qualitative value or of normal or prescribed size or quantity. Commonly used and accepted as an authority." If you were to go back and look at an early dictionary, you would find that *standard* actually meant *ideal*. The standard used to judge anything was perfection, not some amorphous sense of averageness. It was that everything got done right every time, not some of the time. During the decades following World War II we apparently felt uncomfortable with the idea that *standard* meant *ideal*. People striving for the ideal would never measure up, so we felt uncomfortable in using that as a standard. We're not clear about the value of using the ideal. The goal that we should be using is perfection. Supervisors who explain standards effectively will tell people they want the job done perfectly. For example, a supervisor might say to an accountant, "I want the numbers to be right all the time, current all the time, and, therefore, available all the time. I want the reports that come out of those numbers to be correct and accurate all the time."

Perfection is the only goal worth having. Obviously, if you have a goal lower than the ideal, the chances of ever reaching the ideal are zero. If you aim for something less than perfect, that is what you will get. A standard that truly reflects the supervisor's needs can be stated as follows: "I expect that when you do your job, you will do it perfectly. Unless you are confronted by external barriers that you didn't put there, such as too much to do, faulty equipment or data, or people who didn't do their jobs as they said they would. In which case I expect you to take actions to minimize the impact of those barriers or challenges. And I expect you to take those actions at a level fully consistent with the development of your job-related skills. Therefore, if I hire you with a certain level of skills, I want you to use them all to meet the barriers or challenges you encounter in getting the job done."

Most people at work, when I describe a standard in those terms, are aware that it's logical. People go to work every day with the expectation they will get certain things done. The moment their day begins, it starts to go astray. What is it that takes it off the target? Barriers or challenges? The majority of our time is spent overcoming barriers, and not discussing that in the evaluation of performance is to ignore a major component in everyone's work life. Supervisors need to be able to express standards for people in their jobs.

I ask many people at meetings or speeches whether they have the responsibility for evaluating performance, and given the nature of my work, the vast majority raise their hands. When I ask how many find performance evaluation to be rewarding, positive, and constructive, the hands go down and laughter erupts. Performance evaluation is a painful ritual that supervisors would avoid if they could. This is true whether the evaluation is formal or informal. In my experience the vast majority of performance evaluations are done late, unless of course, the company presses people to do them all at once, in which case, they do get done—perfunctorily. We avoid what is painful to us, even if we know it is important in the long run.

The need to know standards and to be judged using those standards in a rational system is not being met in the work world today. Moreover, unclear standards lead directly to performance evaluations that are unfair, arbitrary, and unilateral.

Company—Maximum Productivity

The next level of need that the organization has is to maximize its productivity. Because companies tend to experience more turnover or the wrong turnover (the most competent people leave), many companies have trouble meeting their next level of need—to produce a product or service of the highest quality and in the highest possible quantity. People who are only partially trained retard that goal. Most companies would greatly enhance the likelihood of reaching their goals on productivity if they could slow down the unwanted turnover.

Corporate success requires maximized productivity—optimal quality and quantity. It's a need that is impossible to satisfy if you don't have a stable and trained work force.

You would think, given the fact that we've been managing people and organizations for a long time, we would have a ready response to the question: "What is productivity?" Ask a group of managers and their eyes will glaze over. This is not intended as an indictment of American management, but rather as a statement of fact. It would be an indictment if they had been trained and still demonstrated this level of uncertainty. Understanding productivity is part of the foundation of the management job.

Productivity simply stated is output over input. The output can be measured by the number of psychiatric clients seen, or it can be measured by number and acuity of patients in a hospital, or it can be the number of automobiles or microwaves produced, or it can be the number of new software programs that an organization produces. It can be any or all of those things. The ultimate measurement for output in most organizations is revenue achieved through producing the output. Input, on the other hand, is all of the resources it took to produce the output. Those resources are the human resource, the fiscal resource, the capital (equipment) resource, and the physical (real estate) resource. Those are the principal resources. Input is often measured by what it costs to be able to have those resources in the organization.

In most organizations, between 50 to 60 percent of the input cost is allocated to the human resource. Whether the cost is 3 percent or 90 percent, however, the human resource affects overall productivity in a way the other resources cannot. The human resource can squander financial resources, abuse equipment, misuse materials, etc. The point is they are the most important component on the input side of the equation. If you want to have an impact on productivity, look to your people. In order to increase productivity, you need to do one of several things. You can increase output and at the same time sustain input. If you increase the output of a company that currently has output of $100 million and input of $100 million to output of $110 million while sustaining the input at $100 million, you've gone from a productivity measured at 1.0 to a productivity measured at 1.1. You can sustain your output and at the same time reduce input. Today this is called downsizing. It used to be called layoffs. Before that there was probably another term. In any event, it's uncommon, and if it's done in the best possible way, it is done through attrition.

There are other ways of increasing productivity. You can increase the rate of output faster than you increase input. That is probably the healthiest possible way to develop and grow. However, that relationship between the increase in output and the increase in input is critical. On the one hand, if that increase in output is done without a plan, if that growth takes place and there isn't any real sense for how it's all going to be managed, you have chaos and crisis. You have so much of a good thing that you're not able to even come close to keeping up with it. One of my clients, a rather small company of about $25 million in sales, had, in the early days of my association with them, a constant $3 million backlog of orders. During one period of incredible growth that backlog jumped to $30 million. They had so much work ahead of them the people in the organization were not developing and growing at a rate consistent with the way the company was growing. Unplanned and uncontrolled growth is seldom a positive influence. It is normal to be growing faster on the output side than on the input side. Yet, if you grow on the input side at the same rate you grow on the output side, you are simply getting bigger and may not be more profitable or necessarily producing a better-quality product. It's typical to feel as though there's much too much to do.

PRODUCTIVITY ASSESSMENT

What I would like you to do in order to get a handle on the issue of productivity is to respond to seven questions. Each time you respond, I would like you to make an assessment using a number from 1 (low) to 10 (high).

Productivity Question #1: What is the productivity of the people who work for you as a group? That is, taking the people who work for you, and averaging out those people, what is their productivity?

For the purpose of this assessment, productivity is the degree to which your staff is using its current potential. To what extent is the organization realizing all that they currently have as potential in the job they are doing? This assumes they are capable of doing the job they are in. If they are realizing their potential, they are a 10. If they are using none of their potential, they're a 1. I would like you to rate your group on that scale.

Rate your staff: _____.

Productivity Question #2: Using the criteria from question #1, that is, current effectiveness versus current potentiality in the current job, rate your own productivity.

Rate yourself: _____.

Productivity Question #3: Rate yourself as you think the people who work for you would rate you.

Rate yourself as your staff would rate you: ____.

Productivity Question #4: Rate the other people in the organization who have a similar level of responsibility; i.e., the group of people with whom you need a cooperative relationship in order to be successful; the team at your level.

Rate your peers: ____.

Productivity Question #5: Using the same scale, rate your boss.

Rate your boss: ____.

Productivity Question #6: Rate yourself as you think your boss would rate you.

Rate yourself as your boss would rate you: ____.

Productivity Question #7: Rate the people who work for you as you think they would rate themselves.

Rate your staff as they would rate themselves: ____.

I have asked these questions of literally hundreds, maybe thousands, of supervisors over the course of the last ten years. I will use the responses I have received from that group in order to show the significance of both the questions and your responses.

The average response to the first question is 7. When I say to groups, "What does a 7 mean?" they say, "Well, it's better than average, if 5 is average." But it sure isn't ten. In fact, it is 30 percent less than ten. Yet, we've become so jaded by percentages it just doesn't have the kind of impact it used to. Thirty percent means 1-1/2 days a week those people are not as effective as they're capable of being. It would be simple to explain away that 30 percent by saying that people are withholding the effort. I believe people come to work with the intention of doing their best work but get confronted by barriers, sometimes barriers that other people put there, sometimes barriers that events put there.

The most significant contributing force in the loss of potential is barriers—the challenges between people and getting the job done. It's too easy to explain the difference between potential and actual performance by blaming people. I am not interested in generating a discussion about theory X, Y, or Z. I don't see that any of those is particularly helpful for understanding this problem. The problem is people don't have the *opportunity* to deliver their best. The automobile industry is an easy target. Many people believe automobiles come out of our factories with problems because of worker negligence. They believe the automobile workers of America don't want to produce their best. I say it's because they're being confronted daily with impossible barriers in plants and materials and standards that work against excellence in quality. The Japanese have relatively new, automated systems and facilities. We don't. The problem is that we're not able to produce as we should. Can you blame that on people? I suggest instead that you focus your attention, as the ecopreneur does, on the management of barriers. Getting ourselves and other people to deal with those barriers will increase productivity.

There is another relationship between turnover and productivity to consider: the degree to which turnover affects skill levels of average workers. If people are in their jobs for long periods of time, one finds that the work population is basically 100 percent skilled. The only reason skill levels would be less than 100 percent of their potential would be because of barriers. The effect of turnover in the work world, however, is that employees on average are trained at only 50 to 60 percent of their capabilities. Assuming that is true, and that our standard is built on the degree to which they are trained and able to produce, the best one can expect out of them is 100 percent of 60 percent. The real impact of turnover is on productivity. It isn't because it costs us x number of dollars to put an ad in the newspaper, or to pay employment agencies, or the time consumed by supervisors in doing the training. It's that we end up with people who are only trained to an average level of competence. Beyond that level they're confronted by barriers that diminish their productivity capability even further.

The number most frequently given by supervisors for question #2 (Rate yourself) is an 8, which is one number higher than the average rating given by the staff for their supervisors. In other words, we may think we actually work harder. It could be that we put in more hours, and we are equating working hard with actually producing more. One of the ways supervisors show this capacity for growth is through technical competence. Evidence of better than average performance is most often demonstrated by skills in overcoming more barriers than other people can. As a result of a more effective confrontation with barriers, more of our potential is realized.

The response to question #3 (Rate yourself as your staff would rate you) is generally one or two numbers below the response to question #2. The average to question #3 is a 7. Managers and supervisors think they're not giving us credit for all the work we do. When we become supervisors, we take on a series of jobs that are almost invisible. These jobs are the basic responsibilities of management: planning, organizing, staffing, directing, and controlling. The outcome of these jobs isn't as visible as the product of the operational work done by the people who work for us. When we are confronted by the choice of doing operational (hands-on) work, or managerial work, our instinct is to do the operational work. It has a visible, often measurable, result, and there is an immediate payoff in the feeling of accomplishment and the recognition from other people. The managerial work does not get the same response. For example, employees in work groups often see what they're doing as work, and what their supervisors do, such as attending meetings, as something else. People who report to supervisors don't always see the whole job, and don't give supervisors credit for what they do that is unseen. This is the most compelling reason why I am not an advocate of having supervisors evaluated by the people who work for them.

The response to question #4 (Rate your peers) is the most disheartening; it rates below all the others. This appears to indicate a lack of team effectiveness. The collective effect of positive peer relationship is a strong management team. The responses I have been getting suggest more supervisors feel they are overcoming more barriers to using their potential than other members of the management team. The net result is a feeling everyone may be in a harness but some are pulling harder.

For question #5 (Rate your boss), it's not as helpful to give you an average. The responses are bimodal. People either seem to rate their bosses as 8s, 9s, and 10s, or they rate their bosses as 2s, 3s, and 4s. In other words, "My boss is the greatest boss that I've ever worked for." Or, "My boss would do us all a big favor by staying home more often."

The response to question #6 (Rate yourself as your boss would rate you) is normally one below or one above the number we give ourselves. I think I'm an 8 and my boss gives me a 7, which I interpret as meaning my boss doesn't seem to know what I'm doing, or doesn't give me credit for all that I do. When the score is one above, a 9, I feel I'm getting away with something. If my boss only knew what I could do I'd be rated lower.

The response to question #7 (Rate your staff as they would rate themselves) is 9. We think, in the first question, they're a 7, and we think they think, in the seventh question, they're a 9.

There are several pieces of information to evaluate in this brief exercise. If your response to question #1 is not the same as your response to question #7, it suggests the people who work for you have different opinions about their performance than you do. I am using performance here because we must now start to equate maximized individual potential with maximized organization performance. It suggests you and they are not communicating effectively on this issue. The same is true if your responses to numbers two and six are different. If you think you're an 8, and you think your boss thinks you're a 7 or a 9, you are not having effective communication with your boss about your performance.

There are two important things I would like you to get from this bit of introspection on productivity. First, unless all of your numbers were 10, you see some potential to increasing productivity, given the group of people you presently have, and the potential that they currently possess. Second, there may well be differences in the way you view yourself and other people. If that is true, there is need for you to take some action to handle that. It is important to keep in mind this information is not scientific or necessarily derived from fact. It represents your perceptions, your point of view, your attitude. It is, nonetheless, what you believe to be true. And, after all, we are driven by our beliefs.

ECO-CHALLENGE #18

Organizations have the opportunity to learn the lessons of standards management. They can learn to develop standards, express them to the work force, and measure performance by them. The organization can learn to discuss, instruct, and demonstrate the relationships between standards and quality and between quality and customer satisfaction.

Rate your organization on the following scale:

3 — My company is not only unclear about telling people on what basis their performance will be measured, it doesn't have a clear definition of what a standard is and it seldom talks about standards. When standards are discussed they are so unclear or so rigid that they don't take into account obstacles over which the individual has little or no control.

to

9 — My company is able to define its standards and recognize its obligation to measure only that which can be measured and it promotes an open dialogue about standards and provides managers with the technology to develop specific, job-related standards.

| 3 | 4 | 5 | 6 | 7 | 8 | 9 |

In your words, what statement best describes your rating?

_____

_____

EGO-CHALLENGE #20

Ecopreneurs focus on measurable behavior when defining and measuring performance through standards, and avoid discussions about characteristic such as attitude, judgement, initiative, and commitment.

Rate yourself on the following scale:

3 — If you asked the people who work for me on what basis their performance is measured they would not know.

to

9 — People who work for me not only know the basis for their evaluation, they could evaluate their own performance and there would be no substantive difference between the two.

| 3 | 4 | 5 | 6 | 7 | 8 | 9 |

In your words, what statement best describes your rating?

_____

_____

ECO-CHALLENGE #19

Organizations have the opportunity to learn the lessons of productivity. They are aware of its relationship to turnover. They assist managers in determining the degree to which their staff is reaching its potential and in managing the barriers that limit its potential.

Rate your organization on the following scale:

3 — My company has no idea how little of its current potential is actually being realized and measures productivity by outdated, useless criteria.

to

9 — My company is greatly aware of the difference between realized performance and the actual potential of its work force and makes conscious efforts to achieve its potential.

| 3 | 4 | 5 | 6 | 7 | 8 | 9 |

In your words, what statement best describes your rating?

_____

_____

EGO-CHALLENGE #21

Ecopreneurs know the productivity potential of their staff. They differentiate between obstacles put in their own way and those put there by forces outside the individual's control.

Rate yourself on the following scale:

3 — I have no real impact on either productivity on the company level or potential on the individual level.

to

9 — I am clear that my efforts make a difference on organizational productivity. My staff and I talk regularly about ways to maximize their potential.

| 3 | 4 | 5 | 6 | 7 | 8 | 9 |

In your words, what statement best describes your rating?

_____

_____

PARTICIPATION/CONTROL

People—Participation

Beyond a clearly defined job, fair compensation, and the need to know performance standards is the need for individuals to participate; specifically, to participate in the changes that affect them and to be able to make contributions to the evolution of their own job. It constantly amazes me that people who are at work eight to ten hours a day, who are thinking of better ways of doing those jobs, and coming up with better ways of doing their jobs, are not being asked by anybody how their jobs can be made better and how more can come from their jobs. It is incredible and it is true. The other reason that participation is critical is that people at work today are experiencing enormous change. Their reaction to the change is resistance, and the only way through that resistance is to participate.

What stops people, as supervisors, from getting the participation of the people who work for them? The number-one response for supervisors is, "I don't have the time. It would be nice to take the time, but I don't have the time to involve the people upfront in all these things." The number-two reason participation doesn't happen frequently is that the supervisor, who also hasn't participated, gets the change the same time it must be implemented.

Change is the predominant fact of personal, and corporate, life. Our natural and instinctive reaction to change is resistance. Forty or fifty years ago, we were effective managers of change. Of course, change occurred at a much more manageable rate. Today's rate of change requires more flexibility and commitment from management and employees. Commitment requires participation.

Company—Control

Because people lack expressed goals, and companies lack a stated mission, the possibility for developing effective standards for either is reduced enormously. This frequently leads to a focus on those things that are not working, and a tendency to learn through trial and error, which causes companies to lose the thing that they need next—control. They are losing control over the major resources of the organization. Companies need to control the resources associated with doing business not in the sense of manipulation, but rather in the sense of managerial responsibility to the employees, customers, the public in general, and owners or shareholders in particular.

So what is it that they are trying to control? Basically they are trying to control money and people. The money is controlled through an instrument called a budget, and an attempt is made to control the people through policies, procedures, and management.

If the first two levels of needs are not being met (that is, a stable and trained work force and efficient productivity), controls tend to be brought down on people as opposed to working through them. Policies are developed and administered in a way that allows little or no room for options. Policies are seen and interpreted as though they were rules, not guidelines. Budgets are developed and given to managers, as opposed to being developed by the people who will need to be held accountable for them. It is at the control level that employees typically begin to feel the first sign of overt corporate dominance. If the work force is not sufficiently stable (the company may be keeping the right number of people, while the best talent is leaving), effective productivity is down and control is taken from the individual.

I am convinced that companies don't want to behave in this manner. Companies feel driven to force demands on others. At a time when the company is putting more pressure on, the individual is moving deeper into the realization that their more important needs are not being met.

ECO-CHALLENGE #20

Companies can learn the lesson of participation. The alternative is to experience increased turnover and confrontation through resistance to critical change, change which is ever present, and resistance which leads to diminished productivity.

Rate your organization on the following scale:

3 — My company thinks participative management is one of those theories invented by people like the author of this book to solve nonexistent problems.

to

9 — My company measures the effectiveness of management in terms of productivity and not on the methods used to achieve it. There is freedom to manage as one wishes.

| 3 | 4 | 5 | 6 | 7 | 8 | 9 |

In your words, what statement best describes your rating?

_____

_____

EGO-CHALLENGE #22

Ecopreneurs know the importance of involving people affected by changes in the implementation of those changes.

Rate yourself on the following scale:
3 — The pace is so fast here there is no time for participation.
to
9 — I put the time in upfront for participation and save the downtime caused by turnover and other forms of resistance.

| 3 | 4 | 5 | 6 | 7 | 8 | 9 |

In your words, what statement best describes your rating?

_____

_____

ECO-CHALLENGE #21

Organizations can learn the importance of putting controls at the lowest possible level—the level of the individual. In doing so, they simply acknowledge the truth about where the power resides.

Rate your organization on the following scale:
3 — My company thinks policies are a way to control people and management is told to interpret them very conservatively. Money is controlled at the highest level.
to
9 — My company expresses policies as guidelines for "normal" conditions and it puts budgetary responsibility, both for the development and implementation, at the lowest possible level.

| 3 | 4 | 5 | 6 | 7 | 8 | 9 |

In your words, what statement best describes your rating?

_____

_____

EGO-CHALLENGE #23

Ecopreneurs are aware they have control only as people who work for them give it to them. They know it is not something that can be extracted from people by force.

Rate yourself on the following scale:

   3 — The people who work for me are aware that I have no control over anything except them—they do what they are told.

   to

   9 — The people who work for me know I control both productivity and budgets through their efforts because I tell them so.

3	4	5	6	7	8	9

In your words, what statement best describes your rating?

_____

_____

RECOGNITION/STRUCTURE

People—Recognition

The next need that individuals have is recognition. What many people get instead of recognition is the constant feeling that whatever it is they're doing it is not enough. They leave at the end of the week having the feeling it simply wasn't enough. People need to know they are respected for what they do each day, week, month, and year. They need to have recognition in detail. This is normally done through a process called performance evaluation, which is one of the least effective tools used by supervisors. Ask supervisors about performance evaluation and their eyes glaze over once again. The most common problem organizations have with performance evaluation is they are done late. When a performance evaluation is done late it is saying to the employee, "You are not important!" There are a whole series of things that need to be done competently in order to do a performance evaluation effectively. We've got to tell people with clarity what their job is, and then we need to let them know what the performance standards are for the job.

We need to gather data during a work year to be able to give people specific, effective feedback. The people in most organizations that get the performance evaluations of least value are the best people. They get glib, wishy-washy statements having to do with "another great year," "don't know what we'd do without you," "thanks for being here." They don't get specifics.

People hear glibness if they're the very best employees. Some of the best work we do in performance evaluation is with the losers. We dot i's, we cross t's, we're really clear with them. We tend not to be very clear about what makes a successful person really successful. We have put the spotlight on the losers and the winners are walking around in the shadows. Ecopreneurs know this and do something about it.

Company—Structure

The next level of need that a company has is to structure the company in a way to meet its goal. If the mission is unclear, if the organization doesn't have particularly motivated employees, if the stability is affected, if the productivity isn't as high as it needs to be and the control of resources is marginal, then the company really is constantly trying to do something through a structure that is reactive to the circumstances rather than proactive. The basic building block of the structure of an organization in almost all the organizations that I've been associated with is either missing or deficient. That basic building block, like the atom, is essential to understanding the structure of the company. The basic building block of an organization is a job description. People at work need to know, with some clarity, what their job is. We write three- or four-page descriptions describing the job in ways no one experiences it. It is a description best used for the purposes of compensation. When you ask people to describe what's in their job descriptions, they laugh at you as though to say, "Do you really expect me to remember that?" As a consequence, people are disempowered at work because they can't describe with ease what they do. Organizations respond to questions about job descriptions with one of two answers: "They're being rewritten because they're out of date." Or, "We really don't have job descriptions." A few organizations will say that they have effective job descriptions. Again, the basic structure, the basic building block of the organization, is its job descriptions.

I'm not a fanatic about putting a description in place that is rigid, as you will see later in this book. It is essential the job be defined in a way that the critical elements are clear to the individual and supervisor alike. When people "fail" at their job it is often because they are being successful at the wrong job. They are doing the job they believe to be their job. They are not, however, doing the job their supervisor has in mind. They often disagree on even the critical elements of the job, and, if they get that right between them, they will be out of sync on exactly what it is that the employees are to do about each of those critical elements of the job.

On a somewhat more global level, the structure of the organization relates to the actual reporting relationships, that is, the CEO at the top, and then the Vice-President, and then the Directors, and then the Division Heads, and Departments Heads, and Supervisors, and the Leads, and the people . . . you know, your typical organizational structure.

It is essential that the way the company is organized be consistent with demands from without and within. For example, many companies that were once "product driven" (make a product and sell it) are now "market driven" (make a product and modify it, sometimes dramatically to suit the buyers' specific needs). This provides for considerable external responsiveness and requires great internal flexibility. In order to respond to market pressures, companies will start to press people to do "what the job requires" and it looks as though it wants mindless agreement.

If, as a company, you are product driven, the traditional structure works fairly well. If you are market driven, or even a combination of market and product driven, the old line structure doesn't seem to work. The traditional style of management structure tends to build in turf issues—"my turf, my people, my activity." A sense of ownership of particular portions of the company generates anything but flexibility.

The structure needed here is a matrix. In a matrix structure, people report to a functional manager in their area of expertise and report to a project manager (often several at a time) for different tasks in order to produce to the specific requirements of the customer.

The structure of the organization also needs to reflect what the organization is attempting to do, whether it is a traditional hierarchical structure, a matrix structure, or a matrix structure sitting on top of a hierarchical structure. Generally, structure and reporting relationships are confusing. Some companies want to have horizontal management; that is, everybody reporting to the President, everybody having a sense of being able to make the kind of contribution to the company that is at the level of the Vice-President. That's a wonderful concept when you're still in somebody's garage and developing the company in the early stages. It is not a particularly beneficial concept when you get down to needing to respond to growth issues and consumer issues. If you've got the only product in town, if you've got a unique product, if you're well ahead of your competition, it doesn't make any difference how you're structured. It doesn't make any difference *if* you're structured. However, the more you get into competitive relationships to the world, the more these issues become important.

As in most organizations, by the time you get to where the stability of the work force isn't all that great and the productivity is being hampered by trying to produce through barriers with people who aren't fully trained to do the job, the control of the basic resources is slipping fast. The structure is unclear because they don't have time to be clear about people's jobs, and they're not really sure how to structure or to meet the needs of the market. The cumulative effect of not managing the basics is inevitable.

ECO-CHALLENGE #22

Organizations can learn the importance of recognition. They give considerable visibility to performance evaluation and they hold supervisors accountable for doing an effective job in performance evaluation by measuring the degree to which they are effective as a significant part of the supervisor's own evaluation, thus giving performance evaluation the priority it deserves.

Rate your organization on the following scale:

3 — My company gives only lip service to performance evaluation as evidenced by the fact that there is no consequence if they are done late and sometimes not done at all.

to

9 — My company includes performance evaluation as a significant measure of each supervisor's performance, and supervisors are trained thoroughly in the whole range of activities associated with performance evaluation.

| 3 | 4 | 5 | 6 | 7 | 8 | 9 |

In your words, what statement best describes your rating?

_____

_____

EGO-CHALLENGE #24

Ecopreneurs know that performance evaluation is the central management activity between them and their staff. They know it is not merely an annual hurdle to be jumped. It is a daily, weekly, monthly, disciplined process, and, therefore their staff is seldom surprised by their performance evaluation.

Rate yourself on the following scale:

3 — I find performance evaluation a major pain in the neck.

to

9 — I find performance evaluation both positive and constructive and a significant communication tool for feedback from my staff. I have no resistance to talking to my staff about their performance.

| 3 | 4 | 5 | 6 | 7 | 8 | 9 |

In your words, what statement best describes your rating?

_____

_____

ECO-CHALLENGE #23

Organizations can learn the relationship of organizational structure to the outcome of the company's goals. Job descriptions are clear and current and the overall structure reflects the need for flexibility in responding to the market.

Rate your organization on the following scale:
3 — The structure of my company has no rhyme or reason.
to
9 — The structure of my company is designed to meet the needs and demands of the consumer. Job descriptions are current.

| 3 | 4 | 5 | 6 | 7 | 8 | 9 |

In your words, what statement best describes your rating?

_____

_____

EGO-CHALLENGE #25

Ecopreneurs know that people who can remember the critical elements of their job are empowered, and that it is important to make certain that there is understanding of, if not agreement on, those critical elements between employee and supervisor.

Rate yourself on the following scale:
3 — Most of the job descriptions for the people who work for me either don't exist or are out of date or someone else wrote them.
to
9 — The job descriptions for my staff are current and are frequently part of the conversation about performance. The interrelationship between jobs in my area of responsibility and the relationship to the organizational mission is understood by all.

| 3 | 4 | 5 | 6 | 7 | 8 | 9 |

In your words, what statement best describes your rating?

_____

_____

GROWTH/PLANNING

People—Growth

The ultimate need of individuals and organizations is also highly compatible—the person's need to grow and the company's need to plan. Growth for the individual doesn't always mean a bigger job. It almost always includes the idea of a better life. That better life can include the same job. Many companies, often fast-growing, high-tech companies, have put a premium on fast growth and in the process churned through and burned out a lot of extraordinary talent. The critical factor about growth is that all growth occurs through individual effort. We must take our lead from the individual. When asked what they need in order to experience growth in their own terms, they don't know—a condition directly connected to the lack of personal goals.

This is probably one of the most confrontational activities at work today. People at work are no longer defining all of their growth at work. They will say, "Look, I'm delighted to come here, I enjoy working here. This is not my life, it's simply where I work. My life and my growth is somewhere else." I can remember my father, during his many years as a mechanic, being asked if he wanted to be the service manager. He kept saying, "No." I've got to tell you as a young man I didn't really fully understand why he didn't take the opportunity. My father new instinctively that his growth was in being the best mechanic. He was an extraordinarily good mechanic. He probably would have been a failure as a service manager. The fact that he had the skills to identify problems would have been linked to an incredibly short fuse. He kept saying no, because he knew where his growth was. People today want growth in promotion. Yes, they want growth in another job, they want growth in better work, they want growth in money, they want growth in all those things associated with work, and they want other things. Our job as supervisors is to contribute to that.

Company—Planning

Companies need to plan. Without a plan, organizations don't have a very strong relationship to the future. The future is visualized and attained through planning. Companies without a clear mission strive to have motivated employees, yet put the responsibility for that motivation on the supervisor rather than on the individual, where it belongs. They experience turnover at a rate that is not healthy, diminishing the stability of work force, which has a direct impact on the capacity of the organization to produce. The control of the resources is taken out of the hands of the company, which means there isn't any time to put the kind of structure together to respond to either the individual's needs or the consumer's needs, leaving no time to plan. And since there isn't any time to plan, the company tends to manage in crisis. Crisis management is not the result of a conscious design. Crisis management falls out of not handling other needs.

ECO-CHALLENGE #24

Organizations can learn to maintain a vital work force by supporting the growth needs of their most important resource—people.

Rate your organization on the following scale:

3 — My company uses people and then dumps them when it is done with them.

to

9 — My company knows that individual growth is essential for organizational growth.

| 3 | 4 | 5 | 6 | 7 | 8 | 9 |

In your words, what statement best describes your rating?

_____

_____

EGO-CHALLENGE #26

Ecopreneurs discuss personal and job goals and objectives with their staff.

Rate yourself on the following scale:

3 — I don't talk about any personal stuff with the people who work for me. I don't think I should. I've never learned how, and if I did they would probably leave.

to

9 — I assist my staff in both developing and achieving their goals for growth.

| 3 | 4 | 5 | 6 | 7 | 8 | 9 |

In your words, what statement best describes your rating?

_____

_____

ECO-CHALLENGE #25

Organizations can discover the energy associated with the alliance of mission with plans and goals. It is the only tool that can be counted on to provide security and direction consistently.

Rate your organization on the following scale:

3 — My company operates in crisis management most of the time.

to

9 — My company operates through skillfully developed and expressed plans and has objectives and activities required to achieve them.

| 3 | 4 | 5 | 6 | 7 | 8 | 9 |

In your words, what statement best describes your rating?

_____

_____

EGO-CHALLENGE #27

Ecopreneurs relate organizational planning and goals to the specific requirements of their activities and the day-to-day responsibilities of their staff.

Rate yourself on the following scale:
3 — People who work for me do not know how or if their efforts relate to the future of the company.
to
9 — People who work for me are totally aware of the relationship between their efforts and the future of the company because we talk about it regularly.

| 3 | 4 | 5 | 6 | 7 | 8 | 9 |

In your words, what statement best describes your rating?

_____

_____

Summary

All the needs are compatible. Supervisors have the responsibility to see that people are paid fairly, or at least they understand how their pay relates to other people. They need to let employees know what the performance standards are, need to give people an opportunity to participate, and need to provide recognition in order for the ultimate need to occur—growth. Not as the supervisor defines growth, but growth as the employee experiences it (Figure 11).

The supervisor's principal relationship to corporate needs is being clear about mission, understanding who motivates whom, stabilizing the turnover as much as possible, maximizing the productivity by managing barriers and challenges. Supervisors accomplish this by describing the controls through budget and policies, by giving people a clear sense of their job, and by participating in the planning process. In doing that, managers, particularly ecopreneurs, get the job done.

112 *Ecopreneuring: Managing for Results*

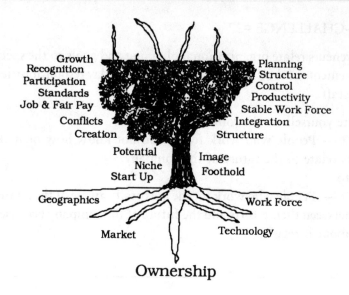

Figure 11

EGO-CHALLENGE #28

Ecopreneurs are aware of the importance of corporate goals and mission and personal philosophy and goals.

Rate yourself on the following scale:

   3 — I have no sense for my philosophy of life and I find the thought of goals confusing and tiresome.

    to

   9 — I am totally committed to my philosophy of life and personal goals.

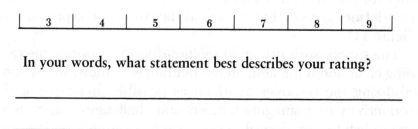

In your words, what statement best describes your rating?

_____

_____

8

Management Ecopreneurial Technology

Primary Goal:
To break down the distinctions that overshadow any real understanding of management styles, management conflict, management stress, and management time

Intermediate Objectives:
To explore the authoritarian, custodial, and participative management styles and give a new set of understandings for all three

To define management conflict in positive, proactive terms

To define a management stress process that is a natural and healthy process

The distinction among management styles, management conflict, management stress, and management time is an illusion.

This illusion was brought about in the decades following World War II. The work world was teeming with people who thought they had a mission to enlighten the work population through its management. Style, conflict, stress, and time are the Four Horsemen of the alliance; that is, the alliance between people and work. To teach time management as a distinct activity and not relate it to style, conflict, and stress is absurd. These circumstances may exist separately in the mind but not the real world. I separate them in this section but their inseparable nature will keep blending their relationships.

The final solution to developing the strongest possible positive relationship to the natural constituents in the ecology of work is in accepting their relationship to one another. The vast majority of people who, when asked to what extent they have been helped by programs on conflict, stress, and time, agree there was little or no long-term affect. The positive, long-term solutions sought in this book will be attained through understanding and reacting to the correlations.

MANAGEMENT STYLES

Primary Goal:
To define the authentic nature of the styles of management appropriate at all the major levels of management

Intermediate Objectives:
To define authoritative, custodial, and participative management

To relate styles and behavior to the requirements of the job and break down the idea of a singular, ideal style of management

The fundamental concepts of style are built on certain preconceived ideas. How we view something sets the tone for our understanding. The perceptions and the tone we have been using to look at style and behavior have been woefully inaccurate. They have not only been wrong they have been harmful. We have been guilty of attempting to homogenize managers into an "ideal" style or set of behaviors. The implication is that all management circumstances require pretty much the same thing. People have been sent to sensitivity and T-group "training," often in an idyllic setting by the ocean and totally alien to the one the person works in. The managers get "sensitized" and returned. They have seen the light and been saved from the evil behaviors they once exhibited.

If you follow the behavior of these people one of two things occurs. They either revert to their old ways or they find it so difficult to continue they leave or fail. The problem is in the underlying assumptions—all jobs require certain humanistic behaviors and certain things, such as using power, are wrong or bad. A person's style or behavior can best be defined by knowing the style that fits the job and working deliberately from that style should be the basis for all the actions of managers. The perspective which I choose to use as the foundation for the purposes of viewing and assessing management styles and behavior is:

> It is not appropriate to homogenize all managers into a style because there is no such thing as a generic, ideal management style.

If that premise is accurate, there must be an alternative or a set of alternatives that offers a better chance at understanding and working with this highly important area. We have a tendency to start our search for style in people. We ask them to describe their behavior in meeting the daily activities and stresses at work. Often this is done with the use of an inventory, of which there are literally hundreds on the market. So they find they are inclined to be domineering, passive, power-oriented, results-oriented, conservative, competitive, avoidance-oriented. . . . The list goes on. The next phase is to determine the "right" behaviors and give the person some broad-based guidelines to implement behavior of a "better" style. You would think thirty or forty years of doing this would have taught us something. One of the principal problems is people who have researched this area, for the most part, have been academics. Undoubtedly, you can pick up some of my cynicism and contempt for people who attempt to fix something they really only understand from an intellectual perspective. The work world is intellectual but it is also visceral.

To understand the styles and behaviors you must look at the job first. It is essential to start with the job to determine the style. It is not just a good idea, it is the only way to assess the behavior needed to do the job for the following reason:

> The behavior we exhibit on the job is much more reflective of the nature of the job (not just what we do but also the circumstances surrounding the job) than the innate nature of the person.

You may chose to disagree with that premise. However, I believe I will be able to demonstrate the facts to support it as we go through this section. We control our behavior and we tend to fit it to the circumstances. There is another rather important piece of information:

> We all have a very wide range of behaviors available to us and we choose to use some over others for reasons not always clear to us.

I don't mean to imply that we don't have certain inclinations. Some of us are certainly more introverted, some are more outgoing, some are more empathic, some of us are more greedy, some more loving, some more wistful, some more gluttonous, etc.

There is considerable evidence that certain behaviors dominate certain jobs. All styles have assets and liabilities. Surgeons are ridiculed as poor communicators on issues of feelings and in appearing unconcerned about the "wholeness" of the patient, the CEO for making things happen through power, and the salesperson for being interested only in the sale.

ECO-CHALLENGE #26

Organizations can learn the importance of establishing expectations of behavior or style related to the demands of the job.

Rate your organization on the following scale:

3 — My company seldom concerns itself with the issues of management behavior and when it does it expects everyone to fit a specific mold.

to

9 — My company has assessed the real expectations and requirements of the jobs into which people are put and acknowledges and promotes winning behavior not according to a model in a book but by looking at the job.

| 3 | 4 | 5 | 6 | 7 | 8 | 9 |

In your words, what statement best describes your rating?

_____

_____

EGO-CHALLENGE #29

Ecopreneurs are aware that they have a vast array of possible behaviors and styles and use the appropriate ones to meet the needs of the job.

Rate yourself on the following scale:

3 — The only style that works around here is to look like, behave like, and respond like the boss.

to

9 — I am aware when I am, or anyone reporting to me is, being asked to operate from a style of behavior that in any way jeopardizes the critical elements of the job.

| 3 | 4 | 5 | 6 | 7 | 8 | 9 |

In your words, what statement best describes your rating?

_____

_____

There are probably as many ways of looking at management style as people who have attempted to examine and understand management behavior. Because this is so, I will use the approach that is clearest and simplest and probably oldest. I am using the simplest not because I judge you to be unable to understand the more complex approaches but rather because its simplicity is its virtue. The more elaborate approaches, by definition, allege a level of necessary complexity to this subject that only serves to add another degree of misunderstanding.

Authoritative/Custodial/Participative

The **authoritarian** manager often displays the behavior most often associated with people who manage others. It is signified by the use of power sometimes to the point where it is viewed as force. Authoritarian managers are *one-way communicators.* They tell people what to do. Their communication style is parental, often critically parental. One of the few certainties you will be able to count on is that your ideas, solutions, and suggestions will be met with oppositional behavior. They frequently turn any interchange with others into a win/lose struggle and they intend to win. Their most common hand gesture is shown in Figure 12, as in, "Look, I don't have any time to get into it right now. Just see that it gets done." Sometimes it looks as shown in Figure 13, as in, "If you can't get it done, I'll find someone who can."

This style is commonly found in the behavior of the people at the top of an organization. You can choose to believe that people

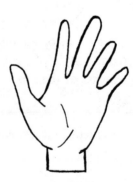

Figure 12

Figure 13

with a strong tendency in the direction of this cluster of behaviors tend to migrate naturally to these jobs or you may want to consider the possibility there is something in the job that brings out this behavior. I say there is something in the job and the environmental imperatives of the job that manifests this behavior. Having been in the management work world for nearly thirty years, I have known literally dozens of people who were certain they would be different when they got to the top and upon reaching that pinnacle of achievement their behavior typically mirrored that which they were certain they did not want to be. What has changed? What is different? Have their values changed? Have their attitudes changed? Have their needs changed? Is it the way they say things? Are they saying the same things and our reactions are now different?

There is a story about a CEO of a company with several locations. One of the locations is so new the CEO has never been there. The CEO has seen pictures, studied the numbers, and approved the deal, but never actually visited the property. Soon after purchasing the property it became necessary for the CEO to visit the new location. The CEO was picked up at the airport by several of the key managers and driven to the facility. The managers were outlining all the virtues of the location. It was in a prime location in both financial terms (rising property values) and in accessibility. It was right off the major freeway for the area. Just as the car was about to exit the freeway one of the managers said, "We own all the land between the highway and the plant." The CEO said, in passing, "Isn't it too bad that small hill is in the way; if it weren't there the building would be visible from the freeway." I think you can guess the remainder of the story. On the CEO's return several months later the hill was gone. The CEO would probably say the comment was simply conversational and not an imperative. The same words said when the CEO was the Vice-President of Marketing would have received a totally different response.

There is something in the nature of the job that naturally leads to this behavior. There is something about being at the top of the organization (Figure 14). First, the idea of it being at the top is an illusion. The CEO reports to someone—unless the CEO, president, and owner are all one person. Generally speaking, there is an individual or a board of directors to whom the person "at the top" reports (Figure 15).

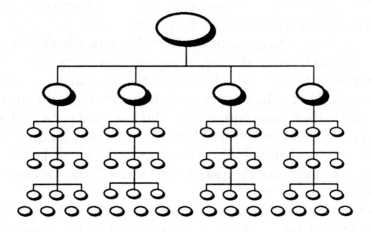

Figure 14

This group is expecting a return on their investment and the actions of the CEO are generally scrutinized to guarantee a successful financial investment. With some companies there is another layer not directly involved, yet with a clearly vested interest. They are the stockholders, municipalities, regulators, and

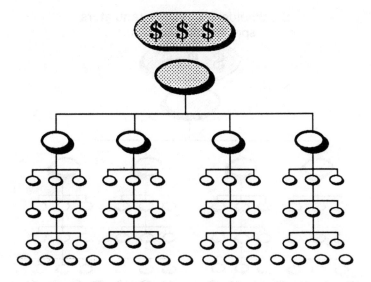

Figure 15

other special interest groups such as the local community (Figure 16). All of these entities can, and often do, exert considerable pressure on the company through its CEO. What comes to the CEO from above are demands. Those demands translate into pressures and those pressures create the highly political nature of the CEO's environment (Figure 17).

Another applicable word to be used to replace politics is *irrational*. That's right, I say the CEO lives in an almost totally irrational world. Think of the kinds of things that come out of the CEO's office. The CEO will ask for something in such a way as to make you think it is a simple and extremely reasonable request. Yet, from your perspective, it often looks insane.

Keep in mind that we have not yet reached the real top of the hierarchy. There is one more and final layer—the consumer (Figure 18). I hope that it is obvious that the CEO is not at the top of anything, but really in the middle. In fact, the CEO in many organizations is the most vulnerable of all the people who work in those organizations.

Beyond the pressure of being in the middle, what is it that causes the CEOs to operate in the authoritarian style? I have said

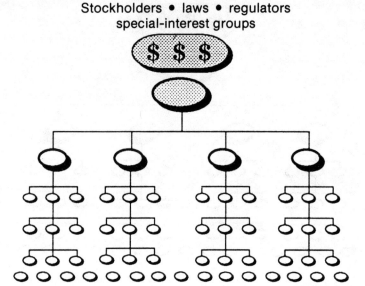

Figure 16

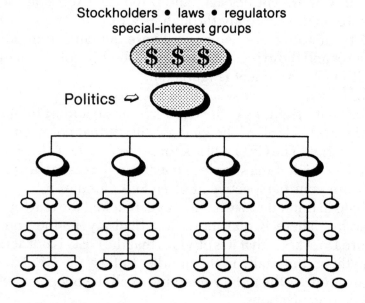

Figure 17

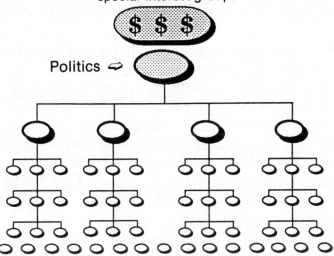

Figure 18

it is common to see CEOs operate out of power. I mean power, not force. Perhaps it would be appropriate for me to make a disclaimer now; it is one I will make several times, because in my hundreds of interchanges with people on this topic I have found it is quickly forgotten. **I am not implying or even suggesting it is ever appropriate for people to carry on in dehumanizing, vindictive, or illegal behavior.** There is in my mind a clear difference between power and force. One is assertive and aggressive and the other is coercive. What does power mean in this context? It is the CEO's assertion that it will get done. This is a person whose vision is almost exclusively in the future. CEOs do care about today and yesterday but only as predictors of the future. CEOs certainly do not care to get bogged down in the petty problems that people have with getting the job done. So when CEOs look to the present they look for the information that will support their contention that the future is in hand.

Sometimes the assertion will become aggressive. Since CEOs are responsible for the future in the minds of the ownership, they are expected to pursue goals aggressively to ensure the future. Being aggressive is part of the job. Being assertive is the intent to make the aggressive goals of the company materialize. Using power is the most convenient and reliable way to make that assertion a reality, not only because other people can't be counted on, which is often the case with the current work habits of many managers, but also because it is the simplicity of action and the conservation of effort that make it at all possible for people "at the top" to move with great agility from one major event to the next.

There is also a distinction that needs to be made in the actions of those in this role between truth and integrity. Allan Bloom, in his book *The Closing of the American Mind*, writes the only thing all young American college students can be counted on to believe is that truth is relative. This is true of nearly all CEOs I have met. The idealist or perfectionist might say, "Nay, nay, truth is truth." I have been in dozens, maybe hundreds, of situations where I was with the CEO of an organization listening to an untruth (notice I have trouble calling it a lie) and knowing it was the CEO's only responsible alternative. A lie has a malicious intent. It is designed to make a loser out of someone. Again, the CEO is in the middle between employees on the one hand and the ownership and customer on the other. Suppose a company is in the thinking stages of a possible downsizing. Does the CEO acknowledge the possibility and in the process unnecessarily worry people and perhaps jeopardize the health and future of the company by having the best talent leave? The best talent will leave because they have the easiest time finding other employment. I have seen many CEOs wrestle that particular demon. I have seen presidents of companies announce products and product delivery dates that made the marketing and production people gasp. Dr. Land, the progenitor of the Polaroid company, was notorious, in the early days of the company when it fit the kind of company addressed in this book, for announcing products that needed more time to be ready.

The integrity of the company and ultimately the future of the employees should be the focus. If the person you work for is mean spirited and doesn't tell you the truth all the time, that person may still be a good CEO. If, on the other hand, your CEO lacks organizational integrity and is intent on abusing people, there is no room for understanding, so move on. There is no easy yardstick to be applied to the assessment of a CEO. Power is the assertion of an intent. That intent may look stupid from your perspective.

Another of the characteristics of authoritarians is their instinct to use one-way communication. This term means precisely what it says. The communication goes in one direction—from the boss to you. It sounds pretty much like this,

> "Look, it's ten now; I want you to take care of the Adams situation."

You go to ask a question and you get the familiar hand gesture (Figure 19).

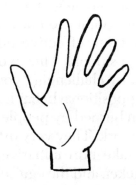

Figure 19

> "I haven't any time to talk to you about it now because I am already late for a meeting. I'll be back about five and I expect to be able to see your assessment and solution at that time."

The boss leaves and I'm wondering if he means John Adams, John Quincy Adams, or Ansel Adams. What is really strange is I will attempt to do what I have apparently been asked to do without any certainty I am going in the right direction.

Why do CEOs use one-way communication so often? It has only one virtue and that's not in getting things done right. On the surface it is a conservation issue; it appears to save time. More often it is used so as not to open the discussion up and demonstrate their ignorance on the issue. The vast majority of the time they don't have the solutions to the problems they give other people to solve. Remember this is a problem in the present and the CEO's attention is on the future. Almost anything needing to be done in the present will be given short shrift. Operating in one-way communications is at once defensive and assertive. It's a defense against exposing their technical and managerial vulnerabilities and an assertion of their expectation of the people in the jobs reporting to them.

CEOs become expert at finding the one wrong number or alternative in a series of correct numbers and solutions, and they don't tend to give credit to people for all the right numbers or proper solutions. They are not negative, they are using the shortest distance between two points. Acknowledging and discussing all the correct data is not time effective. So they get the image of being negative and oppositional. They would say they are looking for your best work by challenging your work. You may not see it that way. Their oppositional behavior is very often learned. That is, they have been burned by people who didn't do it right or didn't do their best work. They very often are waiting for the senior management to take more initiative. This particular problem is the original "chicken and the egg" of upper management. In the early stages the boss has made all the decisions of importance. As the organization grows the boss looks to the senior management to make the move to take control. The assumption is that senior managers are self-starters. These self-starting managers are waiting for the boss to give them the authority consistent with their responsibility. The boss won't give up control to people until they demonstrate they can handle it and the managers won't take control until the boss says they can. So there you have it, the most common standoff in all management practice.

It is essential that the organization have a person "at the top" who is totally committed to winning. How would you like to have a CEO with a laissez-faire attitude about the destiny of the company? You want and need an interventionist. You want the CEO to exercise considerable control to ensure the survival of the organization. I don't think it would be all right with you if your CEO was thinking it would be okay if you lose. In the competitive marketplace there is room for everyone "to go for the gold." However, your ability to take a medal depends on your ability to bring out your best and your intent to get to the wire first.

How many major mistakes are CEOs allowed to make? Their mistakes can cost people their jobs and the company its future. Surgeons, as I said earlier, have the reputation for being much like the CEOs I have been describing here. They are egocentric, one-way communicators who are committed almost beyond reason to winning. Why? Were they born that way? Did they have those instincts and somehow all migrated to medicine and in medicine to surgery? Or is it because we won't let them lose? You go to a surgeon and outline your problem; the doctor makes a diagnosis and recommends surgery. You ask if the doctor has much background in that particular operation and the doctor says yes and he or she is willing to "give it a shot." How would that sound? The truth is you want your surgeon fully skilled and able to succeed every time. If we hold others to the standard of an unqualified success every time, we should not be surprised when they are driven to win and have a very high regard for themselves.

The drive to win every time, the political nature of the environment, and the relative dependence most managers have to the final words of their bosses are at the root of the behavior one finds in the people "at the top." Once again, I *am* saying that we ought not be surprised the behavior of the people in the role of the CEO is authoritarian. I *am not* saying we should accept illegal, immoral, or coercive behavior.

There is considerable evidence to support two other assertions about this authoritarian behavior. First, if the primary behaviors of this style are manifested at the level of the CEO, they will be found somewhere at the next level down. Second, if that oppositional, winning behavior isn't evident somewhere, the survival of the organization is greatly jeopardized.

The first assertion is not the most healthy pattern, but it is a survival technique. You have undoubtedly heard the communications indicative of that configuration. The boss is seen as a pussycat; he smiles; he listens; he's accessible. Consequently, people may think they can put things over on him and say things that might offend another CEO. The surrogate authoritarian will often be heard saying, "Don't let his demeanor fool you, you still have to produce to keep your job around here, and if you don't worry about him you better worry about me." Someone, it seems, must take the role of the authoritarian.

My second assertion is one I have arrived at after many years of observation both as an employee and as a consultant. Part of the maturation process requires the development of authoritarian behavior. Many entrepreneurs resist this evolutionary stage. As a result, they have trouble asserting their demands, the company gets to a certain level and without fail either can't grow further or begins to deteriorate. As I asserted in more detail in the section on Management Stages, this is a major turning point in the development of a company.

ECO-CHALLENGE #27

Organizations that are successful generally have leadership that is willing to exercise control through power and the clear intent to win.

Rate your organization on the following scale:

3 — The organization is extremely amorphous; no one makes demands or expresses uncompromising expectations.

to

9 — The need to win is a driving force in the organization, and although the goals are aggressive, everyone is aware of their roles and the consequences for less than expected effort.

| 3 | 4 | 5 | 6 | 7 | 8 | 9 |

In your words, what statement best describes your rating?

_____

_____

EGO-CHALLENGE #30

Ecopreneurs have expectations of their bosses that are consistent with the real environmental imperatives. They will not tolerate a lack of integrity in their leadership but will accept behavior which in other settings would be considered far too demanding.

Rate yourself on the following scale:
   3 — I expect my boss to treat me fairly and behave in a warm, friendly manner.
   to
   9 — The way my boss behaves is not a conditional factor on either my behavior or my performance.

| 3 | 4 | 5 | 6 | 7 | 8 | 9 |

In your words, what statement best describes your rating?

_____

_____

The **custodial**, or **transitional**, style of management is like the authoritative style in many ways. The use of the word *custodial* comes from the distinction of one who has custody—in this case, of the goals and objectives of the organization. It is the style that is most common at the level below the CEO: the vice-presidents, senior managers, and division heads.

This style of management, rather than telling people what to do, sells them on ideas. It is parental in its behavior, and as such tends to be more nurturing than critical. As in the authoritarian style, it depends on one-way communication. Most people who have the role of senior management understand while the custodial style relates to taking responsibility for or having control over, they don't seem to fully understand the concept of custodial management includes cleaning up after. Cleaning up after whom? In this instance, cleaning up after the CEO. The hand gesture that goes with this style typically points to other people, and frequently can be seen to be pointing up, that is, to the CEO in the kind of the gesture that suggests, "It isn't me that's asking you to do this, and I wouldn't ask you to do it if it were up to me, it's the boss that wants it done."

These are the first people who feel the impact of having too much to do. They are the people who ask the boss, "What do you want done?" And in asking that question, they get the universal answer: "The boss wants it all done." When they ask the boss to give them a set of priorities, the boss simply says, "Get it done." At this point something very important has to happen. The priorities for the organization have to take shape, and this group of people has to understand the job is to move from one kind of management style into another. The style that is above them operates out of power. If they operate out of power with the group below them, the group below them will tend to be dependent in their nature; that is, they will keep waiting to be told what to do.

This is the time when significant alteration has to be made to the way people are managed. This turning point is lost on the vast majority of people in the role of senior management. Many people at this level think the right way to manage is to look like, sound like, and behave like the CEO. They continue to wait for the boss to give them a performance evaluation, for example. They are a group that consistently tells me that they haven't been evaluated for a year, or two, or since they've been on the job. The boss is not inclined to do performance evaluations. There must be a reason. I say the CEO doesn't know enough about their specific activities to do a fair and honest evaluation. And, if the boss did, the only thing that would be measured would be results. There would be no room in the CEO's evaluation for the effort they put into their job that didn't produce a result.

The practitioners of this transitional style of custodial management have to accept the lack of information on their performance from their boss, and at the same time be willing and able to give effective performance evaluations for the people who work for them. As a matter of fact, senior management of a company must do their own performance evaluations, submit it to their bosses, sit down and go over their own self-assessment, make certain that there is agreement, and then move on into the future. At the same time, they must turn around and do performance evaluations for the people below them. This doesn't always seem to be fair, but you will notice I don't spend time thinking about fairness. This is simply the way that it is.

This style of management is selling people on ideas, but is not truly open to other people's ideas. Priorities begin to be put on the things that need to be done. Tasks appearing impossible when handed to the senior management begin to take on the form and substance of possibility. If they don't do their job effectively, it sets an example for all the levels below.

The three principal roles in this style of management are (1) to sell people on ideas, (2) to provide priorities, and (3) to move from a power management style to a participative management style. Senior managers must be willing to operate in a way that is different from the CEO. In fact, they must operate not out of willingness to participate, but out of absolute necessity in order to be more effective in their jobs.

In what ways does this style of management sell? Proponents of this style, in effect, give people a sense of what can be done, often at a point where they don't actually believe it. Keep in mind that these managers are getting all of this input, all of these requirements from the CEO, and they're nodding and indicating their willingness to get it done, and frequently they have no idea about how to get it done. Their job is to sell the possibility. Senior managers frequently will do that by telling people they have no other alternative. This actually doesn't come across like it's been sold to somebody, but rather begins to sound like the telling kind of behavior of the authoritarian, and inasmuch as it continues to be a telling type of behavior, it does not represent the kind of transition that needs to take place. When it is sold, it is sold on the basis of understanding the capabilities of the people who are going to do the job, understanding the resources that are needed, and putting all of that together in a way that gets people to see the possibility. Sometimes it has to be given to people in a way that says, "It has to be done because the boss wants it done." The frequency with which that particular approach is used determines the effectiveness of people who manage at this level.

The absolute worst approach managers can take is to discount the boss. That is to say, "I wouldn't ask you to do it if it were me, or if it were up to me." And to throw their lot in with the people who work for them by saying, "I understand your problems. I know it's going to be difficult, maybe impossible, to do this. However, we don't have a choice." The manager who operates in that fashion doesn't understand the job. People at senior management level get paid the kind of money they are paid, get the kind of titles they get, and therefore the kind of respect in the community because their job is hard, not because it's a snap. Not because they've earned it through some kind of seniority. The nature of this kind of transition is difficult. It requires you to be almost schizophrenic. To be directed one way and direct others in another way is extremely hard, but if it weren't hard it would be done at a level that isn't compensated so well.

As previously mentioned, senior management tends to be one way in its communications. They are neither particularly open to ideas nor do they listen to other people's comments. This is because the kind of comments they get have to do with how impossible the job is, how difficult the job is, how the people below are going to be concerned about it, how there will be a morale problem, how there will be dissatisfaction, how there will be sadness or unhappiness. They are quite used to being confronted by people below them who are willing to tell them of the difficulties in getting it done. I think most people in organizations are not aware of how angry that makes people at the top. CEOs get angry when confronted with information like, "People aren't going to like this." They can't process that information. Their entire outlook is into the future. They get angry for two reasons. One, they think their requests should be handled by the people who work for them. Two, they interpret that kind of response as a form of disloyalty and lack of support in their efforts to be successful. Once people fully understand that their happiness at work cannot be linked to the amount of work, the possibilities for success and happiness get much greater.

This group's job isn't to make the people who work for them happy. They must accomplish what the boss wants done. Of course subordinates are saying, "It can't all be done." Yet senior management using this transitional, custodial style of management is simply saying, "Here's what needs to be done." The job of senior management is to look at the resources of the people below them, and establish priorities. Does that always happen? Not often. The transitional style hands off the work and generates a discussion about priorities, resources, expected results, and the consequences all this has on other jobs currently in the queue. All too often work goes to people below without synthesizing, sorting, or prioritizing. In other words, they give it to the people that report to them in much the same way it was given to them by the boss. The level of decision making, that is, the decision making around priorities, has just been pushed down one level. This is a problem because decisions about priorities are being made across a much broader cross section of the company.

They must be willing to allow the people who work for them to manage in a way that is different from the way they manage or are managed. This is very difficult because they have constant pressure from the boss to get it all done. That pressure typically leads managers to want to manage in a time-efficient way, which means getting things done right. They want also to be effective, which means getting the right things done. The most time-efficient style is the authoritarian style of management. The most time-effective style is the participative style. Trying to convince CEO's and senior management people of that is very difficult, particularly if they are now managed in crisis.

ECO-CHALLENGE #28

Organizations need a level of senior management that knows its role is to move from one style of management to another style of management. They know their job is to set priorities, take the apparently impossible and transform it into the probable, and to transform the power exerted on them into the energy necessary to get the work done.

Rate your organization on the following scale:

3 — People in senior management point the finger at everyone else when passing off the work that needs to be done, and frequently blame "it" on the boss.

to

9 — People in senior management take responsibility for establishing priorities and provide clear performance standards.

```
| 3 | 4 | 5 | 6 | 7 | 8 | 9 |
```

In your words, what statement best describes your rating?

_____

_____

EGO-CHALLENGE #31

Ecopreneurs in senior management don't assess response to requested activities by measuring reactions, they determine the effect of doing what is requested and are open to others who need to manage in a different way due to the specific demands at their level of management.

Rate yourself on the following scale:

3 — The people who work for me know that I think it is a waste of time for them to sit down and talk things through at a meeting.

to

9 — People who work for me know that I will judge their performance and not the manner they use to achieve their goals.

```
| 3 | 4 | 5 | 6 | 7 | 8 | 9 |
```

In your words, what statement best describes your rating?

_____

_____

The **participative** management style is essential at the first and middle levels of management. You must understand at the outset that participative management does not mean it's democratic. You don't vote on things. This is not management by consensus. As a supervisor or manager, you have responsibility, ultimately, for the action and decisions that are made in the group. The fact they voted on anything doesn't take you off the hook. So it isn't democratic. It is participatory in the sense that everyone who is managed gets one guarantee: They will be listened to and given credit for ideas used to solve problems, and if something is going to be done they will have an opportunity to talk about it before it is implemented. That is the guarantee. This style uses two-way communication, which means it is heavily focused on giving and getting data. This style is needed at this level because of the amount of change experienced by those they supervise and the natural resistant nature of people. The circumstances in modern organizations demand it. Years ago it wasn't necessary. Fifty years ago, if someone reported to you and you asked them to do something, they wouldn't ask you why. If they did, you'd say, "Because I told you to." Today you ask someone to do something and they want to know why. They feel they have a right to ask. In truth, if you ignore that right you're going to be in trouble.

Change was very slow decades ago. Today, the only thing that people at work can be absolutely certain of is that their jobs will not be the same in the near term, short term, or the next day as they are today.

What is the normal human reaction to change? Resistance. Why do people resist? We don't really know. We only know that it's natural. The truth is that people will resist change even if they know what is coming is better. You are probably aware of people who are in bad relationships. You know and they know that those relationships are bad. Some people in these relationships are actually getting physically abused. Anything would be better. People in those circumstances often will not change. I don't understand it, you don't understand it, it simply is the way that it is.

Participation is the most effective method to convert resistance to commitment, because people participate in those changes that affect their lives or their jobs. This style of management is slower at getting things done, however. It is so much easier to walk up to somebody, tell them to do something, and leave. The upfront time involved in being a participatory manager is greater. Because that time is taken upfront in two-way communications, the problems of one-way communications are avoided.

One major problem associated with participative management is that people think they may participate in deciding *whether* something is going to be done. Generally, the participation is on *how* and not whether things will be done. If the change affects a specific activity, and in that sense is discretionary, there may be participation on whether something will be done. As work comes down through the organization, there is only one thing that should flow back up—data. Again, what tends to flow back up are comments on unhappiness and misgivings. Managers are required to report on the allocation of resources, the priorities used, the work accomplished, and the work deferred. The only way you, as a supervisor, can be faulted is in the application of those resources, and whether you are attacking the right priorities. The discussions are about measurable, objective performance and accomplishment. You must keep in mind the CEO is more receptive, if not excited, to hear what is and isn't going to be done. The CEO will have more trouble faulting you for reporting the utilization of resources and reporting measurable accomplishments, and have considerable opportunity to fault you for reporting morale and unhappiness problems. Keep in mind neither of those two things can be measured. What can be measured are how many people you have, what the other resources are, what the time constraints are, what the money constraints are, and what gets done. Most of us will fare well using those criteria.

ECO-CHALLENGE #29

Organizations experience change at a rate unthought of fifteen or twenty years ago. People's instinctive resistance to change is overcome through participation in the changes affecting them.

Rate your organization on the following scale:

3 — People hear about change when it is about to be implemented and they are expected to adjust without any turmoil.
to
9 — People participate in the changes that affect them in the planning stages when, and if, possible.

| 3 | 4 | 5 | 6 | 7 | 8 | 9 |

In your words, what statement best describes your rating?

_____

_____

EGO-CHALLENGE #32

Ecopreneurs who are in senior management provide for others below them to manage through participation even though the upfront time demands are greater. First-line and middle managers manage through participation in that they focus on facts, ask questions, and listen to the ideas of others.

Rate yourself on the following scale:

3 — I think it is a waste of time to sit around and discuss solutions since I already know what I intend to do the vast majority of the time.
to
9 — I provide for participative management on the issues of how to accomplish tasks and those circumstances when I don't are clearly the exception.

| 3 | 4 | 5 | 6 | 7 | 8 | 9 |

In your words, what statement best describes your rating?

_____

_____

Summary

My goal in this section on management styles has been to present a convincing argument for the assertion that the style a person brings to the job is more a function of the nature, climate, and environment of the job than it is of the person in the job.

Companies must break the chain of power style. The CEO exerts power on the vice presidents, who exert power on the division directors, who exert power on the department managers, who exert power on the supervisors, who exert power on the lead people. This style exerts power right down to the people at the bottom of the organization, who look down hoping to find somebody they can use power on. What do they find? They find no one below them so they act with assumed power with their associates and with their families at home. One of the few ways to be able to gain power is to unionize. People unionized in the 1980s on issues of powerlessness. Fewer people look to unionize because of hours and wages. They unionize because they're being treated in a way that causes them to feel dehumanized.

MANAGEMENT CONFLICT

Primary Goal:
To define the nature and significance of effective management conflict and achieve an understanding that there is more than a semantical difference between management conflict and conflict management

Intermediate Objectives:
To relate management conflict to mission, roles, and performance

To define workable job descriptions built around clear, brief, and concise critical elements

Management conflict comes out of dedication to the mission through a structure that reflects the product, market nature of the company, and the roles (jobs) needed to produce results. Positive conflict is generated in the acquisition and dissemination of factual information through thoughtful and penetrating investigation. Management conflict focuses on a clear expression of the role a person is expected to perform and asks questions and gives data about performance.

The principal form of management conflict is generated from the tension established between the company's mission and goals and the individual's job and the contribution the job makes to the success or failure of the company. For this reason, the primary activities of management conflict are job definition and performance evaluation. This takes the successful managers beyond the others who feel good because they have learned how to have conflict.

Management conflict exists in our relationships with our bosses, our peers, and our staff. This management conflict, which exists between us and our supervisors, is generated through a clear understanding of the expectations they have of us. We are not in conflict with one another, but with failure. Without this, we will spend our time managing the consequences of confusion and, even worse, unexpected disagreement. Managers often are unable to express those expectations in anything but the broadest of terms. We need to describe our jobs and present that description to our bosses for their reactions. The process for developing the clear description of the critical elements of the job is precisely the same as the one we need to use in developing the expectations we have of the people who work for us. This process is described below in detail. This process also must be used in our relationships with our peers. We need to explain what we need from them and give them feedback in measurable terms, both when those needs are satisfied and when they are not.

At the center of all significant management conflict is performance evaluation. Performance evaluation from your boss, to and from your peers, and of the people who work for you. Job descriptions, as they are currently used, are developed for many reasons and only one is incidentally related to performance evaluation. Most job descriptions are developed for job evaluation purposes—establishing internal and external compensation equity. As a consequence, they are long and totally "unrememberable." For the employees in the jobs, they represent no relationship to their daily activities. People at work today are disempowered because they do not have a clear, brief statement or résumé of their positions (as evidenced by people who go through contortions to come up with a tight, accurate statement to put on their résumés).

> People who can't remember, with precision, the critical elements in their jobs have no mutually understood basis for performance evaluation.

The first of the principal activities required in performance evaluation is to reduce, or distill, all jobs to four to six critical elements. A critical element has two components. First is the *result area*—the subject/object of people's efforts, the product or service measured to establish performance effectiveness or that with which or on which one is expected to do something—the active or passive recipients of our actions. For example:

- Receptionist (Generic)
  - Phone
  - Public
  - Security
  - Messages
  - Correspondence
- Management Consultant/Teacher
  - Clients
  - Materials/Books
  - Financial objectives
  - Speeches
  - Students
  - Goals

It is not necessary that the results areas represent 100 percent of the job. The last 5 or 10 percent will take our attention off the essential elements of the job.

The second of the principal activities involves the *actions* expected to produce the results, the nature and kind of effort exerted on the subject/object to produce the expected results. It is important that we pick our words carefully for we are establishing the tone and intent for the measurement of performance. For instance, in our example, what is the Receptionist expected to do about the phone? Answer it? There are all kinds of answers and styles on the phone. We really want the Receptionist to represent us on the phone. Answering the phone is implied in representing but so are several other crucial needs.

The critical elements for the Receptionist are (in 15 words):

- Represent us on the phone
- Greet/serve the public
- Manage/ensure security
- Take/communicate messages
- Produce correspondence

The critical elements for a Consultant/Trainer (Entrepreneur) are (in 17 words):

- Develop/serve clients
- Create/publish materials
- Meet financial objectives
- Perform speeches
- Develop/evaluate students
- Plan/attain goals

At the center of the dilemma of performance evaluation is the form. Many, maybe most, employers use a generic corporate form to evaluate performance. They evaluate such characteristics as Attitude, Initiative, Judgment, and other apparently measurable criteria such as Job Knowledge, Quality of Work, and Quantity of Work. This single, universal form is used in an effort to be consistent and fair. This is a wonderfully egalitarian thought. The motives are pure but the outcome is the mess we are in now. Supervisors using a single form to evaluate performance are criticized for being subjective by the people being evaluated. Because these forms attempt to cover an entire spectrum, they are not right for any particular area.

It is essential to report performance for the organization on a form using common criteria. This is necessary to promote and ensure consistent evaluations and application of merit increases. This process requires two steps. We must evaluate people first against their jobs and then translate that information to the organizational report form.

ECO-CHALLENGE #30

Organizations can learn that the conflict effective management produces comes from clearly and uncompromisingly asserting the needs of the consumer and the company's intention to meet those needs.

Rate your organization on the following scale:
3 — There is nothing positive about the conflict in this organization.
to
9 — This organization's conflict comes from its belief that quality is meeting the requirements of the consumer.

| 3 | 4 | 5 | 6 | 7 | 8 | 9 |

In your words, what statement best describes your rating?

_____

_____

EGO-CHALLENGE #33

Ecopreneurs don't walk away from conflict, they create so much positive tension, which translates into constructive conflict by telling the truth and holding to high standards, there isn't any time for conflict based on the lack of knowledge.

Rate yourself on the following scale:
3 — I do everything possible to avoid all forms of conflict, whatever the source.
to
9 — I keep my staff so well informed there is only time for the conflict around meeting the objectives we have set out.

| 3 | 4 | 5 | 6 | 7 | 8 | 9 |

In your words, what statement best describes your rating?

_____

_____

Summary

Management conflict is the natural product of establishing a goal, determining what needs to be done to reach that goal, allocating responsibilities, judging people's performance, providing feedback, holding people accountable, differentiating clearly between success and failure and providing a consequence for both. We need to judge people's performance against the requirements of their job and then translate that evaluation to the organization's performance evaluation form. Because this is done so poorly in most organizations, we have to live with conflict management.

MANAGEMENT STRESS

Primary Goal:
To explore the nature and impact of management stress and to define a clear distinction between it and stress management

Intermediate Objectives:
To describe organizational level stress

To describe management/employee stress

To define an effective process for expressing and measuring performance standards

To relate barrier management to increased productivity

Is it semantics or is there a difference between management stress and stress management? Stress is really a personal, emotional, physical, psychological chain of reactions to circumstances. Being alive is reacting to things around us. Some of those things we interpret as negative and some as positive. To some extent this is a reflection of our nature, but mostly it's a reflection of environmental experience. If you grew up in Texas where snakes are a natural phenomenon, seeing a snake would not bring on the same stress reaction as it would if you had grown up in the wilderness of Boston, Massachusetts. As you get older these reactions are pretty much involuntary. So when you get into something called stress management, what you're really doing is managing your reactions. You're not actually managing the stress. There are, of course, some people who are actually trying to find a life without stress. I have had to bring this unfortunate news to many, many people. I hope it's not news to you. I apologize if it is. However, to be alive is to be in a relationship with the world where intense stress is possible at almost any time and where certain stress is there all the time. If you were without stress, you would be dead. To be alive is to interact in the physical universe, which is stressful. To get up in the morning, to lift your body from one position to the other position is to put stress on your body. That's where it begins. It begins as physical stress. Some of us, as we get older, actually experience as we get up in the morning some physical reactions to that stress. And then it simply is a hierarchical activity from the physical to the psychological.

The focus of this section is on understanding that stress is the natural product of management. One of the meanings of *stress* is importance, significance, or emphasis. Management describes importance, determines significance, and gives emphasis to aspects of the job. Management plans, organizes, staffs, directs, and controls in order to place importance, significance, and emphasis on different things at different times. Out of that comes a series of choices and decisions. Those choices and decisions create stress, because in doing one task or project you are, by definition, not doing another. You're never going to follow through on all the choices, so there's stress involved in managing.

The question in management stress is whether or not you're able to put the correct importance, significance, and emphasis on any particular activity at any time. If you pick the less significant things to do, or the less important things to do, or give emphasis to the wrong task, you're creating the wrong kind of management stress.

All significant management stress comes from one of three sources: the ownership, the leadership at the top, and the stress the manager creates. Both ownership and leadership at the top have been discussed in some detail.

The manager creates stress through an unrelenting focus on quality and zero-defect performance. The ecopreneur knows quality is what you have if you don't take anything away. Most people think quality is added to something. The ecopreneur spotlights the things that get in the way of perfect performance. Ecopreneurs don't get into the discussion of Theory X, Y, or Z. They use clear performance standards to transform potential negative stress into positive stress. The energy the employee normally puts into not knowing and apprehension about performance evaluation is converted to a strength to maximize performance and clarify expectations.

> Standards expressed as less than 100 percent, ideal or perfect institutionalize barriers and make maximizing potential impossible, which diminishes both organizational and individual potential and threatens the competitive position.

The proper yardstick is perfection. However, using the ideal, or perfect, doesn't "feel" right because it doesn't seem to be attainable. Attainability is an essential part of any standard. There is a softening or hesitancy to hold people to tough goals. This has probably happened through the misguided belief it is more fair. If the standard doesn't take into account the reality of people's experience in their jobs, it is not only unattainable it is unreasonable.

A standard can be expressed as a simple, one-thought statement, if we are willing to accept the fallout. The simple standard that drives (no pun intended) the auto industry is, "The assembly line must not stop under any circumstances and x number of cars will be produced each hour, day, or week." There is an underlying standard to produce perfect cars but it is subjugated by the simple, one-thought concept about the assembly line. To overcome the lower quality that results, which is a natural outcome, consumers get "recalls" and "7/70" warranties. We assume problems will arise and we will need the warranty (which, of course, we have already paid for).

> If consumers don't expect a product or service to be right the first time, a simple, one-thought standard can be used.

The effective standard most of us must express will have three elements: the goal, the reality test, and the foundation.

1. The goal:
   The critical elements of your job are to be done perfectly/ideally . . .
2. The reality test:
   unless you are confronted by external barriers, in which case, you are expected to take action(s) to minimize the effect of those barriers, . . .
3. The foundation:
   maximizing the development and use of both your job specific and transferable skills development.

The standard, when the three elements are combined, reads as follows:

> The critical elements are to be done perfectly unless you are confronted by external barriers, in which case, you are expected to take actions to minimize the impact of those barriers through the development and use of both your job specific and transferable skills.

When I express this standard in management groups, CEOs make it clear they like the zero-defect reference point and they don't like, or "feel" comfortable with, the reality test. It looks like an opportunity for excuses. People spend much of their time at work overcoming, reacting to, avoiding, or ignoring barriers or obstacles. If performance evaluation ignores the reality of barriers, it will take this activity outside the work world as people experience it. The only barriers allowed to have an impact on the ideal are external barriers or those put there by someone, or something, else. I will take this one step further. Most people, in jobs of all levels of complexity, spend as much time dealing with barriers to getting their job done as in doing their jobs. Consider the thought process you go through on your way to work. You plan your day. You arrive at work and something, sometimes it feels like everything, begins to conspire against your plan. To not focus on barriers and the actions expected to manage them is to ignore a major segment of everyone's day. It also reduces the likelihood of deinstitutionalizing those barriers.

CEOs are measured by the irrational standard that focuses only on their results. Using their standard throughout the organization has led us to our current problems.

> All increases in productivity and the attainment of quality goals are brought about by diminishing or overcoming barriers.

Quality isn't something we put into the product, it is there in the first place. Obstacles diminish quality and productivity. The challenge is always in getting through the obstacles. "Genius," Edison said, "is 1 percent inspiration, 99 percent perspiration." The perspiration comes from constantly and tirelessly confronting barriers. One doesn't design for something to work only part of the time unless you are up against sheer chance. You might design a system to win at blackjack this way, but it is not necessarily a good business strategy.

The six to eight principal barriers and the same number of common actions need to be identified in each job. The standard becomes a point of view. The job is (1) to take actions to overcome barriers, (2) to produce maximum results, and (3) to develop and maximize the use of the skills required in the position. All of these are observable and measurable.

Many barriers remain because we don't know how to resolve them, have an organization that won't address them, or are committed to their presence.

One common barrier reflects a myth in the workplace: If you don't do a good job you will be fired. That simply is not true. In most organizations a person has to work a plan to be fired. People who have failed, or are failing, are not allowed to fail and move on to success somewhere else. We "stash" them and ignore them into oblivion. They remain and represent a serious obstacle to others.

Some barriers aren't worth the effort or expense required to get rid of them. They are part of the culture or we keep forgetting they are there. We must go after all but those where the cost exceeds the return.

Management stress is associated with power and management distress is associated with panic. Panic is associated with crisis management. Crisis management develops as a result to a lack of planning. There is no time to plan because the basic management needs are not being met. The manager is a source of stress. To be alive is to be in stress. All stress is action and reaction. Management stress focuses on actions.

ECO-CHALLENGE #31

Organizations must have a clear mission, define goals and objectives, and target dates for successful attainment of each.

Rate your organization on the following scale:

3 — No one but the boss knows what we are going to do next and the corporate mission is fuzzy, at best, for most people in the organization.

to

9 — The ownership has a clear and articulated mission and each key manager has developed strategies to reach the mission.

3	4	5	6	7	8	9

In your words, what statement best describes your rating?

_____

_____

EGO-CHALLENGE #34

Ecopreneurs, in order to have a balanced view of both their goals and the organization's goals, are aware of the significant sources of personal stress. The result is personal stress that is defined around accurately identifying and articulating the important and significant and putting the proper emphasis of activities and resources to achieve results.

Rate yourself on the following scale:

3 — I react to things as they come to me and have little or no time to think beyond the current set of crises.

to

9 — I place stress on the important and significant through emphasis on their impact to the activities, objectives, goals, and mission of the organization.

| 3 | 4 | 5 | 6 | 7 | 8 | 9 |

In your words, what statement best describes your rating?

_____

_____

Summary

How do ecopreneurs create positive management stress? Management stress ties directly into management time in that it's essential to be able to determine the importance, significance, and emphasis to place on things, and that is linked somehow to the mission and goals and objectives and activities that fall out of that mission. Management stress is created to move toward the management mission. You can see if a company doesn't have a clear sense of mission, the only kind of stress left is stress management; that is, trying to manage the reaction of stress in one's environment.

The organization creates normal, needed stress through the connection of mission to goals to objectives to activities to jobs to tasks. The only clearly measurable element of this hierarchy is the task. It does not work from the top down. As each task is accomplished, the job gets done; as the job gets done, the activities get done, and so on. It is at the level of the task that we have the absolute ability to observe and measure behavior. It is also the level at which any rational standards can be applied. Without clear standards the natural, normal tensions needed to support and guide intention are converted to contention and from there to distress.

Stress is natural. Distress is the natural reaction to confusion and panic. Confusion in one's job is often the result of a lack of clarity about the basis on which one will be judged. Therefore, management stress is healthy tension which exists as people apply themselves fully to their jobs against tough goals and standards in order to achieve a clearly stated mission. Through recognition that includes both evaluation of results and efforts, there exists the possibility for both short- and long-term success (Figure 20).

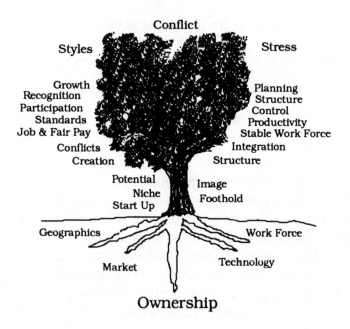

Figure 20

9

Management Ecopreneurial Strategies

Primary Goal:
To provide a clear definition of, and a blueprint for, implementing ecopreneurial management behavior

Intermediate Objectives:
To review perceptive, practical, and attitudinal implications for ecopreneurial management

To review eco-challenges and ego-challenges, stress and communications, and provide a clear understanding of the impact each has on ecopreneurial management

To provide a practical and tangible process for defining positions that empower people at work and a logical, usable approach to performance standards

To review management communications and management time

> To determine basic company and personal needs and provide a system to develop goals to meet those needs

Strategies are implemented on three levels: (1) the perception level, (2) the practical level, and (3) the attitudinal level. This book was designed to provide a view of the work world clear enough to alter your notion of the way you think it should be, ever was, or ever will be. This is not done in a sense of defeat, but rather in the sense of mustering the energy and power available in it and not using up our energy and power in opposition to it. Organizational ecologies change in much the same way as physical ecologies change. This takes place over time and with considerable effort if we attempt to change it faster than it naturally wants to change. I am not saying you cannot change the ecology of your company. I am saying putting your energies there is less likely to be successful than putting them on managing the activity within the context you get. The second approach enables you to manage successfully nearly anywhere. Success in the first approach is preconditioned on changes in the environment and that environment is controlled ultimately by someone else.

THE PERCEPTION LEVEL

Eco-challenges and Ego-challenges

You now have the opportunity to assess your perception of the nature of the ecology in which you work. Keep in mind we are not trying to ascribe good and bad but rather to determine the issues and pressures which you are either currently resisting or giving in to. In the columns below, place the scores for your company for the 31 Eco-challenges to which you responded as you read this book.

Management Ecopreneurial Strategies 153

Eco-challenge #1	_____	Eco-challenge #17	_____
Eco-challenge #2	_____	Eco-challenge #18	_____
Eco-challenge #3	_____	Eco-challenge #19	_____
Eco-challenge #4	_____	Eco-challenge #20	_____
Eco-challenge #5	_____	Eco-challenge #21	_____
Eco-challenge #6	_____	Eco-challenge #22	_____
Eco-challenge #7	_____	Eco-challenge #23	_____
Eco-challenge #8	_____	Eco-challenge #24	_____
Eco-challenge #9	_____	Eco-challenge #25	_____
Eco-challenge #10	_____	Eco-challenge #26	_____
Eco-challenge #11	_____	Eco-challenge #27	_____
Eco-challenge #12	_____	Eco-challenge #28	_____
Eco-challenge #13	_____	Eco-challenge #29	_____
Eco-challenge #14	_____	Eco-challenge #30	_____
Eco-challenge #15	_____	Eco-challenge #31	_____
Eco-challenge #16	_____	Total	_____

How is your company doing overall? If your responses are in the range below the midpoint (the lowest possible score is 93 and the highest is 279, therefore the midpoint is 186), it is apparent you are not in an ecology supportive to natural, positive management. In all likelihood, this means you are in a typical work environment. The inclination of the company behavior on the lower end of the scale can range from hostile or indifferent to neutral or mildly interested in the development of a healthy ecology.

Your reaction to the ecology you are in determines your effectiveness. It is imperative that you analyze the degree to which you are resisting the relatively fixed nature of your company. Certainly you must determine whether you are presently attempting to change elements in the ecology of your company over which you have little or no control. To determine areas of possible significant contention, please look to those on the lower end of each of the individual eco-challenges. Judge each of them on the basis of the following:

1. Is this something over which I have enough control to change it?

2. What steps have I been taking to alter the impact of this ecological reality?
3. How does this affect my productivity and that of the people I manage? How does it affect my management time and that of those around me? Are there specific and measurable negative effects on daily, weekly, and monthly productivity? Are periods of time lost to complaining and general griping?
4. Is this something that confronts my basic moral and ethical principles?

Again, the successful manager and certainly all successful ecopreneurs place effort in areas where they have some control and report the impact, in factual terms, of the ecological influences on those they do not control. If you look at the issues a review of the eco-challenges raises and feel or think it would be easier to go somewhere where it is "better," you may want to keep in mind it is not better anywhere else, it is only different. Ecopreneurs change jobs for one of two major reasons. It is the next step to accomplish their goals or it is because they find themselves in an environment that operates at a level of moral, legal, or ethical conduct that conflicts with their principles. When ecopreneurs are interviewed for new positions and asked why they are leaving their current jobs, the responses are connected to the future and future goals and not to the past and past problems.

In order to determine the impact the nature of the ecology described above has had on you, please place the responses you gave to the 34 Ego-challenges in the column below. You may feel you have been less affected by the ecological requisites of your organization than you, in fact, have been. If you are not certain you have been completely truthful about yourself in your responses, you may want to ask one or two people whose judgment you trust to respond to the 34 ego-challenges from their perception of you. *Truthful* may be too strong a word. *Accurate* may be a better choice of words. It is not easy to ascribe negative characteristics or behaviors to ourselves. Ecopreneurs are aware, however, that the last person they want to fool is themselves.

Ego-challenge #1	_____	Ego-challenge #19	_____
Ego-challenge #2	_____	Ego-challenge #20	_____
Ego-challenge #3	_____	Ego-challenge #21	_____
Ego-challenge #4	_____	Ego-challenge #22	_____
Ego-challenge #5	_____	Ego-challenge #23	_____
Ego-challenge #6	_____	Ego-challenge #24	_____
Ego-challenge #7	_____	Ego-challenge #25	_____
Ego-challenge #8	_____	Ego-challenge #26	_____
Ego-challenge #9	_____	Ego-challenge #27	_____
Ego-challenge #10	_____	Ego-challenge #28	_____
Ego-challenge #11	_____	Ego-challenge #29	_____
Ego-challenge #12	_____	Ego-challenge #30	_____
Ego-challenge #13	_____	Ego-challenge #31	_____
Ego-challenge #14	_____	Ego-challenge #32	_____
Ego-challenge #15	_____	Ego-challenge #33	_____
Ego-challenge #16	_____	Ego-challenge #34	_____
Ego-challenge #17	_____		
Ego-challenge #18	_____	Total	_____

What does it look like for you? The lowest score was 102, the highest score was 306, and the mean score was 204. Ecopreneurs are in the upper range of the scale. If you are not there, don't fret. Take solace in knowing you can move to a more successful relationship than your current environment by adopting and mirroring the attitude and behavior of the ecopreneur. To take on the attitude a conscious decision must be made to go against the natural flow created by the ecological nature of your organization. The behavior of successful managers has been described in each of the ego-challenges. After we have gathered some more significant data, we will consider some useful strategies for the implementation of these changes. Ecopreneurs know that space in their lives (that is, areas that are unmanaged), will tend to be filled by whatever is most abundant in the environment or ecology. The truth of this is evidenced by our behavior when we need a break. We take a vacation, turn our management behavior off, and go somewhere where the natural influences are not indifferent or hostile to us. The elements most available in the typical work environment are not positive. They are certainly not waiting for you to come along in order to support you. Much of this book has been dedicated to describing the influences in the normal business ecology. The skillful ecopreneur knows that stepping back, taking a break, or taking it as it comes is a mistake in the world of work.

You need to assess the areas where you are not exhibiting the behavior of an ecopreneur. There are three obvious areas—personal management, people management, and environmental management.

Company Stress and Personal Stress

The information mentioned above is both interesting and useful, because much of its use is on a thinking level. In order to assess both your company and yourself on a more visceral level as you relate to your ecology, it would be helpful to look at the information from the stress inventories.

Company stress

The ownership establishes the context for stress reactions. Please respond to the inventory below to establish the stress climate of your organization.

Respond as you believe it is today, and as you think it was in the past. If the statement "Ownership has a positive image of the company" is almost always true, put a 1 in the Present column. If it is generally true, put a 2 there. If it is seldom true, put a 3 there. And then, before you move on to the next statement, put a number indicating whether it was almost always true, generally true, or seldom true in the past.

Directions—Please indicate whether each of these statements is

    1 — Almost always true
    2 — Generally true
    3 — Seldom true

for both the *present* and the *past*.

	PRESENT	PAST
1. Ownership has a positive image of the company	_____	_____
Consumers have a positive image of the company	_____	_____
Management has a positive image of the company	_____	_____
2. Ownership trusts management and employees	_____	_____
Consumers trust company to provide for its needs	_____	_____
Management trusts both ownership and employees	_____	_____
3. Company has a secure competitive position	_____	_____
Company's competitive strength is due to past	_____	_____
Competition is viewed as positive and healthy	_____	_____
4. Product/service meets all customers' expectations	_____	_____
Flexibility allows for quick response to customers	_____	_____

All are committed to 100% customer satisfaction _____ _____

5.
Change is seen only as new challenge _____ _____

Growth is planned, positive, and exciting _____ _____

Priorities are resolved so the pace is managed _____ _____

6.
Standards of excellence are expressed for all _____ _____

Standards focus on results and efforts _____ _____

Observable behavior is measured as performance _____ _____

7.
Corporate objectives are clear and expressed _____ _____

Departmental activities tie directly to objectives _____ _____

Job descriptions are clear and expressed _____ _____

8.
Future is forecast with clarity _____ _____

Company has short- and long-term plans _____ _____

Company is excited about the future _____ _____

9.
Mission describes relationship with the customers _____ _____

Mission describes relationship to
competition   _____   _____

Mission describes relationship to employees   _____   _____

                           Totals   _____   _____

Please take the totals for your company's relationship to stress and put them below.

    Past _____   Present _____   Future __?__

In order to predict the future it is essential to have these two pieces of information. Keep in mind the lower the number the more positive the relationship to stress. In what direction is your company headed? If the number is going up, there is movement in the direction of more negative reaction to stress. If the number is going down, there will likely be more positive reactions to stress in the future. If the numbers are basically unchanged, it will be the same in the future. Ecopreneurs may know they may have little opportunity to change the direction if it is negative, but they do know strategies are needed to operate effectively within the company stress environment. Now, place below the totals from the Present column for each of the nine groups of three. The past information was only needed to produce a prediction about the future, and because it is in the past it is not available for change in the present in any event.

1. _____ **Company Image**
   How does the company impress others?
   Whose standards are being used?
2. _____ **Trust**
   Who does the company trust completely?
   Does the company take risks in order to grow?
3. _____ **Competitive Position**
   Is the company in a powerful competitive position?
   Is the company one of a kind?

4. _____ **Product/Service Acceptance**
   Does the company get positive product acceptance?
   Do people care enough to tell?
5. _____ **Pace**
   Can the company slow down whenever it wants to?
   Is the pace managed?
6. _____ **Standards**
   Is perfect or ideal the goal of company standards?
   Do standards reflect both effort and results?
7. _____ **Objectives**
   Does the company express clear, measurable goals?
   Are they clear to those expected to attain them?
8. _____ **Planning**
   Does the company forecast effectively?
   Is planning a high priority?
9. _____ **Mission**
   Is the mission expressed clearly?
   Is it clear to those expected to achieve them?

If any of these areas has a score of six or below it suggests it is an area of current potential distress for the company. Some of these sources of potential stress are focused in the past (company image, trust), some are focused in the present (competitive position, product acceptance, pace, and standards) and some are focused in the future (objectives, planning, and mission). Besides the obvious implications inherent in a less than positive relationship to any of the specific areas above, there is a significant impact on the company's use of time. This will become more apparent as you review your own stress.

Personal stress

Ecopreneurs are aware to what extent they are handling the personal stresses in their life. Below is an inventory, similar to the one for your company, for you to assess your current level of personal stress.

Directions—Please indicate whether each of these statements is

    1 — Almost always true
    2 — Generally true
    3 — Seldom true

for both the *present* and the *past*.

	PRESENT	PAST
1.		
I feel good about myself and take care of myself	_____	_____
I am comfortable about myself as a person	_____	_____
My interactions with people are "free and easy"	_____	_____
2.		
I have friendships that are close and trusting	_____	_____
I have others, whom I trust, to talk to when I wish	_____	_____
I make close friends even though I may get hurt	_____	_____
3.		
I feel at ease talking to a wide variety of people	_____	_____
I have a sense of teamwork on my job	_____	_____
I feel I work with others to achieve goals	_____	_____
4.		
My parents do/did accept me for the person I am	_____	_____
People important to me love me unconditionally	_____	_____

Most people respond positively to me _____ _____

5.
I handle difficult situations calmly _____ _____

Doing my best is all I expect when I compete _____ _____

I can relax whenever I want to _____ _____

6.
I use time effectively _____ _____

I accept change and the problems it can create _____ _____

I am not concerned about the past or the future _____ _____

7.
My work is satisfying _____ _____

My work is secure _____ _____

My work allows me to be the way I really am _____ _____

8.
Life is exciting for me _____ _____

I look to the future with enthusiasm _____ _____

I am where I want to be in terms of my growth _____ _____

9.
I do what I want though others don't always approve _____ _____

I am basically honest with myself _____ _____

My life is taking the direction I want it to _____ _____

10.
My personal goals are as clear as they need to be _____ _____

I am comfortable with my job goals   _____   _____

My job goals are consistent with my
life goals   _____   _____

                              Totals _____   _____

Please take the totals for your relationship to stress and put them below.

Past ____   Present ____   Future __?__

What does it suggest about your stress level in the future? If the numbers are going down in the direction of the future, keep doing whatever you are doing. If those numbers are going up, some behavioral and attitudinal changes are needed.

Now, once again distribute the subtotals from the Present column of your assessment of you.

1. _____ **Self-Image**
   How do I impress others?
   Whose standards am I using?
2. _____ **Trust**
   Who in my life do I trust completely?
   Do I take risks in order to grow?
3. _____ **Consonance**
   Do I feel a bond with other people?
   Do I feel isolated or am I a part of a team?
4. _____ **Acceptance**
   Do people around me accept me as I am?
   If I fail, will they still care?
5. _____ **Relaxation**
   Can I slow down whenever I want to?
   What is the hurry?
6. _____ **Time Management**
   Can I stay focused in the present?
   Do I think about the past or worry about the future?

7. _____ **Job Satisfaction**
   Am I generally happy in my work?
   Am I different at work?
8. _____ **Growth**
   Do I know what my potential is?
   Am I working a plan to get there?
9. _____ **Control**
   Do I control my life or do others?
   Have I given up control or has it been taken away?
10. _____ **Goals**
    Do I have a plan for my life?
    Do I understand how goals are developed?

Now let's take that information and see what it suggests about the kind of personal stress you are living with. The first step in this process is to do what I call a reality test, and that is to find out how are you doing in general. If we know the past and we know the present, we have the capability of predicting the future. If your number goes up from the past to the present, it means you are handling stress less well now than you did in the past. That is, the more responses that you answered with "seldom true," the higher your number. All of the statements in the preceding inventory are positive statements about how one is handling stress in their life in ten different arenas, so to say "seldom true" is to say that it isn't so in your life, and that it doesn't represent a positive force for you. If your number goes down, it suggests exactly the opposite, that is, you're handling stress better now than you did in the past. Certainly a total of 60 or above suggests that at this point in your life there's more stress that is distressful to you than stress that is positive for you.

Well that's all well and good, but we can't really attack these kinds of issues effectively by looking at them from the broad picture. So what are the areas that we've been looking at? You now have numbers for self-image, trust, consonance, acceptance, relaxation, time management, job satisfaction, growth, control, and goals. When you find a six or above on this scale, it says that, on balance, there is more stress in this area that is distressful than is positive.

So what is self-image? What are we talking about here? This is an arena that for most people at this point in the development of our country is very difficult not to have stress in. We are surrounded by media that suggest all of us should be thirty pounds lighter, be taller, have a full head of hair, not have dandruff, not smell, as a matter of fact, we've got an American image of people that is almost depersonalized. It's almost nonhuman. It is something out of a box. In any event, almost all of us have some questions about how we are perceived by others. Questions that we're generally asking ourselves here are: How do other people perceive us? What's really important here is, how do we perceive ourselves, and what standards are we using in order to develop that perception? Self-image is the basis from which we operate. The ecopreneur manages the self not so much by focusing on self, but by focusing on measured success.

The next area of potential stress is trust. Trust is significant in our relationships with others, both at work and at home. If we don't trust, we don't risk. If we don't risk, we don't grow. If we don't grow, it is clear that we're not going to reach our potential. Often in life we find ourselves in situations where we've extended ourselves. We've put ourselves out there for somebody else and they have let us down. And sometimes that causes us to decide that we're not going to trust other people, which means we're also not going to ask other people for things we want. We are going to have to do it all ourselves, which also means we're not going to get what we need in life. I'm sure you know people, as I do, who have spent their lives not asking. The only problem with not asking is that you have the satisfaction of not asking, and the dissatisfaction of never getting. It's like the person in a relationship who says, "If he really loved me he wouldn't need to be asked. I don't want to ask him." So they don't ask, they don't get.

The next area is consonance. Consonance has to do with the degree to which we feel a part of what's going on around us. Do we feel a bond with other people? Do we feel isolated? Do we feel part of a team?

Acceptance is probably the most clinical of the issues that are on this list. Acceptance is something that goes back to our roots—our childhood. Did, or do, our parents accept us for the persons we are? I have an associate who, using nearly any standard imaginable, is successful. However, he consistently walks around with this feeling that he never quite made it, because his family, his parents in particular, don't really accept the way he's been successful. They perceived him as being a doctor. He ended up being successful in business.

Relaxation is a ubiquitous problem in our country. Americans don't seem to know how to relax. They'll drive their automobiles at speeds that in no way relate to their need to get from one place to another. Maybe you've not had this experience, but most of us had. We're driving fast, and we had this thought, "I'm not really in a hurry." And we're still unable to slow down.

Time management is an area that I'll get back to after I've had a chance to discuss the remaining areas.

Job satisfaction is pretty evident. If it's below six it generally means you're finding some satisfaction in your job. If it is six or above it implies you're not finding the kind of satisfaction you're looking for on your job. Again, there should be no big surprises here for you, because you are either clear you're generally happy at work, and you're true to yourself, or you feel you're actually having to be substantially different than who you are.

The area of growth has to do with your sense that you are a dynamic, developing person. Frequently, as is true with the rest of ecology, growth comes from being in the light, not in the darkness. Growth is in direct relation to the experience one has of being aware of one's environment, moving into one's environment, and developing what one's possibilities are.

The next area questions the degree to which we control, or other people control, our lives. Now, no one has a life where they totally control it, or at least I haven't met that person. To live is to give up control. You get into an automobile, you give up certain controls. You accept certain things, such as wearing your seat belt or stopping at the stop sign or driving at the rate that is acceptable by law. The question here is: Has control been taken from us? Did we give control to somebody else? When we marry, we give up some control; that is, we either share control with someone else, or actually give it to someone else. When children come along, the control shifts again. We can't do all the things we did before, so the issue of control is: Did I give it up? Am I conscious of having made that decision, or did somebody take it from me?

Goals are just exactly what they suggest. If you have a high number in goals, it suggests you need to have a plan for your life and you don't. To need goals and to not have goals is to be frustrated. The effect of the negative implications of our relationship to stress can be seen best in its effect on time.

Management Behavior

Primary Goal:
To provide an opportunity to assess the real demands of the job in order to determine the appropriate management style, communications, and time

In order to establish the appropriate behavior and style for you in your job, it is essential to determine the environmental and personal factors influencing the effective performance of your job. It is important that you and your boss be in sync on these factors. Otherwise you will be behaving in a way consistent with your understanding and your boss will be looking for behavior consistent with his or her view of your job.

The following inventory is not intended to represent all of the significant behavioral components but rather a representative sampling. You may want to assess your job and ask your boss to do the same thing. The most important outcome of the exercise is the dialogue that it will generate between you and your boss. Should you find other factors or components, all the better. The factors are juxtaposed as a way to force choice. They are not necessarily opposites. Your job may, at different times, require all of the action or approaches in the inventory. It is precisely because of this that you are asked to choose between them and establish different degrees of importance.

Job components

On the lists below, check off only one in each set.

Example

    __X__ Tasks greater than time   ____ Tasks equal to or less than time

Environmental factors

- ____ Tasks greater than time available
- ____ Tasks equal to or less than time available

- ____ Priorities clear
- ____ Priorities unclear

- ____ Priorities changing
- ____ Priorities static

- ____ Standards unreachable
- ____ Standards reachable

- ____ 100% commitment required
- ____ Time for outside interest

- ____ Expected to win every time
- ____ Big win occasionally

- ____ Consumers wants unreasonable
- ____ Consumers wants achievable

- ____ Transactions mostly outside of company
- ____ Transactions mostly inside of company

Personal factors

- ____ Self-starter
- ____ Take direction

- ____ Unconventional
- ____ Follow procedures

- ____ Independent
- ____ Responsive

____ Single-minded   ____ Multifaceted

____ Individualistic   ____ Team player

____ Confrontational   ____ Humanistic

____ Results oriented   ____ People oriented

____ Constant winner   ____ Willing to lose

Now take the list of eight chosen factors from each of the two lists, environmental and personal, and prioritize them. The most important factor is 1 and so on.

Environmental

____ Big win occasionally

____ Consumers wants unreasonable

____ Consumers wants achievable

____ Expected to win every time

____ 100% commitment required

____ Priorities changing

____ Priorities clear

____ Priorities unclear

____ Priorities static

____ Tasks equal to or less than time

____ Tasks greater than time

____ Time for outside interest

____ Transactions mostly inside

____ Transactions mostly outside

____ Standards reachable

____ Standards unreachable

Personal

____ Confrontational

____ Constant winner

____ Follow procedures

____ Humanistic

____ Independent

____ Individualistic

____ Multifaceted

____ People oriented

____ Responsive

____ Results oriented

____ Self-starter

____ Single-mindedness

____ Take direction

____ Team player

____ Unconventional

____ Willing to lose

Ecopreneurs bring the right kind of behavior or thinking to the job as determined by the nature of the job, not simply by the title of the job.

Management Communications

> **Primary Goal:**
> To demonstrate that each person is aware of the appropriate nature of management communications

Communications is probably one of the most mysterious of all the skills or issues that one needs to deal with in this process of exploring management. There are countless programs designed to enhance one's communication skills. We are taught to listen better, to explain better what it is we expect, to focus on certain issues and not on others, to tell the truth in a situation. Despite the technologies available, communications is typically the most serious problem in the average relationship. As a consultant, I can go to almost any company, talk to no one, go in the front door, walk through the organization, go to the office of the chief executive, have that person say to me, "What do you think are our serious problems?" and if I were to say, "Communications," I would be right most of the time. There is something about communication that is incredibly elusive. It is because we try to treat communication as a separate entity that we run into this problem. Communication needs to be addressed as it relates to the other things, so it will be most helpful for us to look at communication as it relates to the style of management that we have, or communications within the arena of conflict and stress.

In this section on management communication, I will focus on the premise of communications—the transactional nature of communication. Ecopreneurs understand both the effect the nature of their communication has on others and the instinctive reaction they have to other people's communication premise. My use of the work premise may not be clear since it is not generally applied to the behavior associated with communication.

In all our communications we operate from certain assumptions or presumptions. They represent the premise for the communication behavior that follows it. Presumptions are made about environmental and personal circumstances. The principal environmental factors are demands, time, direction, and priority. The principal personal factors are emotions, intellect, and stamina.

Once the factors are sorted out, the premise is established. For most people this all happens with little or no thought and little or no intervention. I am eager for you to examine the underlying premises you use in your communications and the consequences they produce on others and, more important, on you.

In each of the five situations that follow choose the one response that you believe to be the most *appropriate* response. I am specific in the use of the word appropriate. I am not asking you to respond as you think you would, or as you would like to, but rather as you believe it is appropriate. Put an X next to the response you feel, think, and believe to be most appropriate. After you have identified the most appropriate of the responses to the situations, please put an X next to the second most appropriate response. You will have two X's for each of the situations. One that represents the most appropriate, and the second that represents the second most appropriate. You don't need to differentiate between those two. That differentiation will become apparent as you go through the assessment process.

1. Your boss calls you and wants you to attend an hour-long, unscheduled meeting. You are in the midst of an urgent project that has to be completed by 4 P.M. You can't do both so you
    a. get angry and try to get out of attending.
    b. agree to attend without any reference to the urgent project.

    c. say you need to plan better. You can do one but not both.
    d. remind the boss of the project and look for a compromise.
2. A person who works for you has lost (misplaced) a file. This is the fifth time this month this has happened. You say,
    a. "This has happened several times, is there a problem you need to discuss?"
    b. "I hope you won't be upset but I really wonder if you know what you are doing?"
    c. "Oh, for God's sake why can't you ever keep track of simple things like papers?"
    d. "Damn it all, I needed those papers right away and now I don't know what I'm going to do."
3. One of your peers at work comes to your office upset. He says, "Jack tells me that you have been giving him work without going through me. I feel we ought to get things straightened out." You say,
    a. "There was one time when I discussed a project with him when you weren't in. Were there other specific times?"
    b. "I guess I did step into your bailiwick somewhat. I'm awfully sorry."
    c. "Let me tell you something. Someone has got to make some decisions. I saw a need and moved to meet it."
    d. "You're always accusing me of something. I wish to hell you'd cut it out."
4. A vice-president, not your boss, says "College students are inspired by communists. Don't you agree?" You say,
    a. "Yes sir, I agree with you. It's a serious mess."
    b. "I sense that there are highly complex causes for student attitudes. What specific data are you using?"
    c. "It's not caused by the communists at all. You should read what I've been reading."
    d. "I wish I were back there now. I sure wouldn't stand on the sidelines this time."

5. One of your peers at work stops by and says, "Stan's being shoved out of the VP slot—some kind of shake up—and Jane is going to get the VP job." You say,
   a. "It really bugs me the way people come and go here. Jane gets the job and she's no better than Stan."
   b. "Well, that's not my business. What's that really got to do with me at my level?"
   c. "Why don't they do the decent thing and let the person resign? It's all a big political game anyhow."
   d. "This is the first I've heard about it. Where did you hear all this?"

Please take your responses and put them on the response collector below. Find the letter a, b, c, or d and put your X in the space provided, then add up the number of X's in each of the columns.

1. c. _____   d. _____   a. _____   b. _____
2. c. _____   a. _____   d. _____   b. _____
3. c. _____   a. _____   d. _____   b. _____
4. c. _____   b. _____   d. _____   a. _____
5. c. _____   d. _____   a. _____   b. _____

Totals _____(A) _____(B) _____(C) _____(D)

You no doubt see some consistency in your responses. Your highest number is most likely in the column second from the left. The behavior associated with that choice is participation, problem solving, reality testing, and asking questions and giving information (data). You know instinctively the way to best accomplish your communication objectives is to use these behaviors. You often don't and the consequences of not doing so may contribute more to individual burnout than any other factor in your work life. This will be explored more thoroughly later in this book.

Personal Communication

Please distribute your responses (the totals from above) to the communication inventory below.

Critic _____ (A) Tell/Sell Make Judgments Make Statements Give Opinions	**Participator** _____ (B) Solve Problems Reality Test Ask Questions Provide Data
Rebel _____ (C) Resist/Create Get Angry Act Aggressively Operate/Feelings	**Adapter** _____ (D) Comply/Accept Feel Controlled Withdraw/Avoid/Agree Suppress Feelings

The behavior associated with each of the communications options are shown below the total for each. As I mentioned earlier, you probably see the benefits associated with the behavior in the **participator** column. You may remember I asked you to respond as you thought it would be appropriate to respond. Some of you may be thinking there were other responses you would have liked to use or you feel you would have used. In truth, we behave at work in the manner we feel is appropriate. It may well be true at home you would have told your spouse to put a string on his glasses to find them in the future or storm out of the dentist's office in a flurry of angry remarks. One of the major premises of the book is that we are different in different arenas in life. People behave at work in a manner they might not at home. Generally, that manner is more controlled and "appropriate." The positive, constructive, problem-solving behavior we see as appropriate is also most available to us when we are in reflective moods and relatively stress-free environments. As you have seen, your work environment is anything but stress free. In fact, some management stress is needed to create the atmosphere for creativity and results.

The behavior associated with your next highest total is likely the behavior you exhibit when you are under pressure, which for some of us is most of the time. Although there is no certainty, the direction I describe is your direction; it is the course of action most people take. For the majority of managers I have worked with the next highest number is in the **adapter** column. They adapt to, comply with, and accept the pressures. This adaptation, compliance, and acceptance is not necessarily accompanied with a feeling of goodwill. It is out of a feeling, or sense, of being controlled. The behavior is to agree, though perhaps not be in agreement, and sometimes withdrawal and avoidance.

The struggle in life is to stay in a positive communications premise. That is, the way to resolve anything is through information and questions. The move to being adaptive is predicated on the premise, "I have no power." Some people go to the **critic** column directly following the participative behavior. This style of behavior is premised on the belief, "I know better." It is the style of the authoritative manager and sometimes the transitional manager. As you can see, their communication process is either to tell or sell; their reactions are defensive. They make judgments and state opinions. Managers who operate from this style will have people who report to them who operate from the adapter style. You can predict, with some certainty, the response you will get to your style. Either the rebel or the adapter will get the critic style in response. The critic will almost certainly get either the rebel or the adapter. The rebel behavior is the last refuge for all communications. It is the final response most people use, though it may be the first one to come to mind and feeling. When we are confronted by the critical nature of a person or organization, our first reactions are to resist, get angry, take aggressive actions, and resolve the feeling coursing through us. Of course, at work we do not do this. As a result, we are behaving one way and feeling another. This duality is significant and extremely unhealthy.

The process goes something like this. We are at the job and are told to do something or be somewhere or have something done. We really don't want to have anything to do with it but we smile and say, "Sure, I'll handle it. You can count on me." Under our breath we are saying, "you dirty son of a ..." The consequences of being driven to a behavior unlike the one we would refer is devastating.

An example may help to show the significance of this reaction. Imagine you are on your way home. You are in a hurry, of course you are always in a hurry. You stop at a grocery store to pick up a few things. As you leave the store, bundles in arms, you push the door just before you read the sign that says "pull." You react. This reaction is not apparent on the outside. It is an internal reaction. The reaction can range from rage to moderate disturbance depending on the kind of day you have had. At that moment, your body gets a shot of adrenaline. Adrenaline's purpose, in this instance, is to give you extra physical capacity to fight or flee. When you pull the door, generally with a little flourish, you use up the adrenaline.

Please translate those circumstances and your reaction on the job. Even though on the outside you are smiling, the adrenaline is flowing. It is responding to your internal reaction. Unlike the situation at the door, this adrenaline is not being used. It is being stored. Adrenaline has no positive value in our lives beyond fighting and fleeing. Stored adrenaline is like fused dynamite looking for a match. We smile and nod our way through the day and start dumping our adrenaline on the highway on the way home, or we keep it in control until we get home and look out. Spilled milk will take on the significance of a world problem; your child won't understand and neither will you. People who feel pushed and prodded to actions and behaviors other than the ones they wish are likely to experience burnout. Burnout is actually burn up.

Ecopreneurs have two strategies they use to ameliorate the potential hazards of these pressures. They are aware of their natural pattern of movement through the communication premises. They make that movement with thought and condition it to the circumstances. If they are in control and are the only source of information, they may operate as the critic while recognizing the impact it will have on others. When solutions are needed and they do not hold all the information, they will operate in a participative way. When the control is in someone else's hands, they acknowledge the obvious and move to adaptive behavior without bringing along the emotional baggage. Since this is very hard to do, they employ a second technology to handle the accumulation of adrenaline. If they live on the West Coast they either meditate, exercise, or both. On the East Coast they exercise. When I ask supervisors on the East Coast about meditation, they look at me as though I were crazy. Either activity will do. The average American will work the kind of day I have described, go home, have a drink, eat a big meal, watch television (on average more than 27 hours a week), and go to bed. They are not using up the adrenaline and it needs to be used up. People who exercise know there are benefits beyond the physical ones. They feel better and more in control of their lives. If you want to know if you are in need of reducing your adrenaline level there is one simple test. When you wake in the morning, are you rested? If you are not, it is probably because you have a heightened level of adrenaline. The body doesn't want to store it, so there will be a consequence of not using it. Not all ecopreneurs are exercise fanatics—most are not. They simply find a safe, simple exercise they enjoy doing and stick to it. The researchers say walking is one of the best. I am personally an avid nonjogger. I jogged for a while and found it incredibly boring and unsocial. I like to walk and bike and I do both with people I like. When the circumstances require, I use a stationary bike inside.

This exploration of communications was intended to provide you with a rational approach to others and to your own needs. You have undoubtedly observed I have given rather short shrift to the rebel behavior. I wanted to save it for last. You will notice stuck in the middle of a lot of apparently negative behavior is creativity. Creativity is the child of rebellion. There is no creativity in the critic, who is more interested in his or her belief, or the adapter, who is more interested in his or her feelings. All significant advances in human history, when first expressed, were met with critical review because they looked crazy. What response did Columbus, Marconi, Einstein, and hundreds more get to their assertions? To be creative is to rebel; to rebel not against someone, but to rebel against implied and expressed limitation and alternatives. Ecopreneurs are creative problem solvers, and as such have access to the rebel in themselves. They will consider any and all alternatives before selecting a course of action. The rebel in us needs to be available when the old solutions won't cut it anymore. The premise for this behavior is, "We need a truly creative solution or idea."

Ecopreneurs move through the communications styles with understanding and ease. Not because they are forced to, but because they bring the right premise to the task at hand.

Management Time

> **Primary Goal:**
> To explore the basics of management time and its focus on the present

Management time isn't a matter of dealing with the finite. It is style, conflict, stress, mission, planning, objectives, activities, and priorities. Management time is what you have left after management styles, management conflict, and management stress are either understood and effectively implemented or not. Management time is also an attitude. It is skillfully maintaining a focus in the present.

Once again, let me make the disclaimer that I have made several times throughout this section. I am not in any way suggesting that it is appropriate for supervisors, managers, directors, vice-presidents, or CEOs to behave in ways that are patently dehumanizing or abusive.

Is there really such a thing as management time as opposed to time management, or is it really semantics? We've been trying for the last two or three decades to teach people something called time management. We've also been working to teach people something called stress management, and conflict management, and we actually haven't been very successful at any of those things. I think the principal difference between the concept of management time and time management is that management time starts from the concept of the big issue, and works its way down to the smaller issues. Time management starts from the small and works its way to the big. It assumes that if you do the little things right, the big things will take care of themselves. Management time, on the other hand, is designed around doing the big things right. We don't manage time. We manage what we do in the process of the inexorable movement of time. If you think you can manage time, look at your watch, slow it down, speed it up, or stop it.

The basic premise in management time starts with the keen understanding of the mission of the organization. That mission can be stated in different ways; however, each manager has to take that mission inside and be able to connect directly to it through the efforts of that individual. When effective, management time is also connected to personal goals. Effective managers connect the mission of the organization to their personal goals in life, to the point where they are so connected as to generate enthusiasm and power out of that connection. Effective ecopreneurs manage time through the effective implementation of planning to accomplish the mission of the organization. I'm going to take this from the big issue and work my way through to the small issue. Most people, when you ask them how many hours there are in a week, think about work time in the week—40 hours, 48 hours, 50 hours. Almost no one, when you ask that question, can tell you that there are 168 hours in a week. I don't know why, but it's true. The point is that when we have an approach to management that starts from the big and knows that number, as the manager knows the mission of the organization, we actually have a construct in which we can work.

There are 168 hours in a week. The average person works somewhere around 50 to 60 of those hours, including going to work, being at work, and returning from work. That does not include the time at home thinking about work. But for most people, you can use 60 hours as the number of hours committed to that thing that we call "labor at work," and that leaves 108 hours. Again, the average person sleeps about 7 hours a night, and so there's about 50 hours consumed in the activity of sleeping, which leaves 58 hours left in the week. Most people cannot actually tell you what they do with those 58 hours. The ecopreneur can tell you what happens to those 58 hours, because they're planned in order to accomplish objectives through activities that have been designed with certain priorities. This is the flow of management time.

As a sidelight, for the average American, 27-1/2 of those remaining 58 hours are spent in an activity that most people don't want to own up to, but apparently an awful lot of us actually participate in, and that's in watching television. Of course, we say, "No, not me. I don't watch that much television. If I do, I only watch public television." It's awfully easy for a few hours to get consumed in the process of watching television on a daily or weekly basis. In any event, rather than reading, rather than writing, rather than walking, an awful lot of people are spending approximately half of their disposable time watching television. So management time sets priorities to obtain goals that have been planned in order to accomplish a mission. The process works from the top down: First the mission is set, and the rest follows—planning, objectives, activities, priorities, then timing.

Let's return to the issue of management time. Management time and management stress are inextricably connected. To manage stress is to manage time. The ecopreneur creates management time by measuring both personal and management stress. In managing time, the assumption is that we come into the present 100 percent available. I say it's the assumption, because as you will see it isn't actually true.

If we have stress in the areas of self-image, trust, consonance, and acceptance, it is all associated with the past. We got our self-image out of the past. We decided not to trust because of something that happened in the past. We don't feel that consonance because of the way things have been in the past. Our acceptance is from the past. And the degree to which we have stress in these areas represents a drain in the present. When we think about self-image, trust, connectedness, and acceptance, we are generally thinking in negative terms. Those negative terms are focused on guilt—things I should have, could have, or would have done—and blame. Now, it is true that some of our thinking in the past has to do with positive thoughts about the good old days. Those thoughts are fleeting. They come and go, and we use the energy behind them to support the present. However, when we're thinking about the negatives in the past, they are draining us from the present. Conservatively, people spend probably somewhere between 10 and 15 percent of their lives being concerned about the past. That means that without doing anything, people are already working at 85 to 90 percent capacity. The rest is drained off thinking about the past. Of course, it isn't easy to forget the issues of the past. When we get to the strategy section of this book, I will provide you with some alternatives if those areas are of concern to you.

The areas of job satisfaction, growth, control, and goals are all future-oriented stresses. Job dissatisfaction is a problem because you think your work life is going to be the same in the future as it is now. Growth is obviously in the future. Goals are in the future. Control has to do with looking at and believing that it's going to be like this tomorrow. When we think about the future, the most common feeling we have is worry. You know, as I do, that we all worry to some degree. What does worry do about the future? Nothing. Worry does not alter the future one iota. Worrying about the future steals time from the present. Again, let's assume people spend 10 to 15 percent of their time worrying, though truthfully I think that number is probably lower than what we would actually find if we did an in-depth survey on this problem. Before starting to work in the present people are now down to 70 to 75 percent of their potential.

Ecopreneurs manage the past. They have the same kinds of problems in managing the past that others have. Ecopreneurs don't tend to get the magnifying glass out and look for the tack along the road that created the flat in their automobile's tire. They tend to look at the tire, change the tire, and move on. Some people would say that's avoiding.

Ecopreneurs simply don't have the management time to spend looking back for answers. The answers for them are in the future, and in the present. The way ecopreneurs gain time in the present is to stop worrying about the future. The way ecopreneurs do that is to have goals. In order to have goals, ecopreneurs are clear about their needs. Goals stop the worry for the most part, because the daily accomplishment of a worthy goal makes people feel successful. In feeling successful, the worry about the future diminishes. So ecopreneurs become successful in managing time not because they are better, more skilled, more able, brighter, or more intelligent, but simply because there's more of them available in the present.

Time management, on the other hand, teaches us techniques and strategies such as handling a piece of paper only once, or having lists, or operating with written planners. The assumption here is that if we can get the little stuff down, the big stuff will be manageable. Well, if that were true, the vast majority of people sent to time management seminars would be better planners. The fact is, they are not. We have not done an effective job of developing management timing skills. It isn't that people are not competent; organizations haven't taught people what they need to do.

The first thing you need to have in order to be effective in management time is a clear, unquestionable understanding of your organization's mission. Second, a clear understanding and commitment to your own personal goals. Third, an effective plan to accomplish both organizational missions and your own goals, and then develop specific objectives and strategies to meet those missions. Finally, you must combine these three steps into activities dedicated to accomplishing your mission. This generally means that management time is driven by a plan of action. Effective managers, and certainly all ecopreneurs, understand and use action plans.

What is a plan of action? What are its elements? A plan of action starts with an objective, which is tied directly to the organization's mission. An objective is a relatively long-term goal, generally on the order of one to three years. All action plans include a critical path and time commitments. The critical path consists of the activities necessary to accomplish the objective. However, before you determine the timing, you need to determine the activities. People often will establish the completion date and then make the plan fit the timing.

An effective plan of action starts with an objective, and then identifies the activities, or critical path, and the resources necessary to accomplish each of those activities. Each activity has its own objective, which, when met, provides the planner with discrete results leading to the ultimate goal, or mission. Once the time frames are known for each of the discrete activities, then management time decides when the overall mission will begin and when it should be completed.

Does this sound like time management again? I see it as mission management. I see it as goal management; managing the goals and objectives to accomplish the mission. It may seem like I'm playing word games here, but my intent is to take our focus off of the way we use time, deal with the finite, and put our focus on the way we deal with the big picture. How we're dealing with the accomplishment of the organization's mission.

In my experience, I have found that effective managers don't think about time, they think about results. And as you notice, the results are right in the middle of all the activities taking place in the plan of action. People who are effective managers (that is, ecopreneurs) have three major personal behavioral attributes through which they save considerable time. It isn't as though they're out there to manage that time, they simply save time. One of those attributes is that all effective ecopreneurs have goals. In having goals, they save considerable time that others spend wallowing around thinking about where they're going. I will explain this even further in the area having to do with management stress. The second is in the way they manage stress. They're aware that to manage is to create stress. We will look at that in the next section, The Practical Level. There is something about the way they respond to and handle stress that enables them to save a great deal of time.

The third attribute ecopreneurs have is that they don't complain. Of course they have things they could complain about, they just don't complain. And they see fewer things to complain about. In most organizations, if you went through on a day-to-day basis and just listened to groups of people, you would find people sitting around complaining about the way things are. They are typically talking about how their work came to them, how they have too much to do, how they'll never get it all done, how the people who work for them are not content. Even in happy, healthy organizations you will find that there is this kind of attention put on complaining. I believe that about 50 percent of the lost time in organizations can be linked directly to complaining. Complaining about things that ultimately don't change. Complaining that doesn't tend to make any difference as it relates to getting things done. Ecopreneurs don't have time to complain because they exert management time.

THE PRACTICAL LEVEL

On the practical level, I can help you with the technology needed to define jobs in a way that is clear and concise, performance standards that are usable, and the substance of a performance evaluation process designed to work.

Defining the Job

You may recall I described my job earlier in less than twenty words. You need to do that for your job and for the people who work for you. List the four to six results areas in your job—the subject/object of people's efforts, in other words, the product or service measured to establish performance effectiveness.

- Receptionist (Generic)
    Phone
    Public
    Security
    Messages
    Correspondence
- Management Consultant (My job)
    Clients
    Materials/Books
    Financial objectives
    Speeches
    Students
    Goals

- Your Job _____

  _____

  _____

  _____

  _____

  _____

  _____

Define the nature and kind of effort exerted on or to the subject/object to produce expected results. It is important that you pick your words carefully for we are establishing the tone and intent for the measurement of performance. I have listed below several words you may use to express the actions needed. Feel free to use them in the actions for your job but, please, don't feel limited to them. Make a list of several for each result area.

Result Area: _____

Actions: _____

_____

Result Area: _____

Actions: _____

_____

Result Area: _____

Actions: _____

_____

Result Area: _____

Actions: _____

_____

Result Area: _____

Actions: _____

_____

Result Area: _____

Actions: _____

_____

Account	Confirm	Diagnose
Administer	Conserve	Direct
Advise	Consolidate	Discover
Analyze	Construct	Dispense
Arbitrate	Consult	Disprove
Arrange	Control	Distribute
Assemble	Coordinate	Draw Up
Assist	Correspond	Edit
Audit	Counsel	Eliminate
Build	Create	Evaluate
Calculate	Criticize	Examine
Chart	Deliver	Expand
Coach	Design	Find
Collect	Detect	Formulate
Complete	Determine	Identify
Compound	Develop	Implement
Conduct	Devise	Increase

Install	Perform	Render
Institute	Plan	Represent
Instruct	Prepare	Research
Interpret	Prescribe	Restore
Interview	Present	Review
Invent	Process	Route
Judge	Produce	Select
Lead	Promote	Sell
Lecture	Protect	Serve
Log	Provide	Solve
Maintain	Purchase	Speculate
Make	Realize	Sponsor
Manage	Receive	Study
Mediate	Recommend	Supervise
Negotiate	Record	Supply
Obtain	Recruit	Test
Offer	Reduce	Train
Operate	Refer	Translate
Order	Relate	Write
Organize		

Now reduce the list of actions to the best two or three and describe your job below in the following manner:

Example

    My job: Consultant
        Develop and Serve Clients
        Create and Publish Materials
        Meet Financial Objectives
        Perform Speeches
        Develop and Evaluate Students
        Plan and Attain Goals

    My job: _____

_____

_____

_____

_____

_____

_____

Now that you have described your job as you see it, you have half the information needed to be certain you are on solid ground. The next step is to get your boss's input. This is the foundation for all the assessment about your job. Your employees will be empowered with a description they can remember. This same technique I have shown can be used for those who work for you. If you are at a level where you are either not well enough informed to do this for the people who work for you or expect them to describe their jobs themselves, ask them to use this process and then react to what they produce in light of its contribution to department, division, and organizational objectives.

Developing Performance Standards

The next step is to define performance standards. The standard, as stated earlier, is as follows: **The critical elements are to be done perfectly unless you are confronted by external barriers, in which case you are expected to take actions to minimize the impact of those barriers, through the use of both your job specific and transferable skills.**

In order to use this standard, you need to identify the ideal for each of the critical elements, the barriers most likely to interfere, and the actions most needed to reduce the impact of those barriers, and the skills needed in the job.

In defining the ideal, I have noticed people tend to express a comfortable goal or maybe even a challenging goal and not the ideal. In a nurse's (RN) job, for example, the critical element is to develop and manage the patient care plan. The goal, or criteria, often used as a standard is to have the plan in place within 24 hours after patient admission. The ideal is that the plan be developed and available whenever needed, whether it is two hours or twenty hours after admission. To use 24 hours is to account for the barriers to having it in place sooner. In doing this the barriers become blurred and institutionalized. Describe the ideal for each of your critical elements.

Critical Element: _____

Ideal: _____

_____

Critical Element: _____

Ideal: _____

_____

Critical Element: _____

Ideal: _____

_____

Critical Element: _____

Ideal: _____

_____

Critical Element: _____

Ideal: _____

_____

Critical Element: _____

Ideal: _____

_____

As you defined the ideals for your job, you were probably aware there are barriers to reaching the ideal. From the list below, identify the five most significant barriers in doing your job. This list represents the distillation of much input from hundreds of supervisors, though feel free to add your own descriptions.

- Time
- Equipment
- Materials
- Data
- People
    - Commitments Not Met
    - Poor/Fair/Marginal Output
    - Negative Attitudes
    - Communications Problems
    - Inaccessibility
- Team/Group Ineffectiveness
- Unclear Standards
- Changing Priorities
- Change
- Undeveloped Skills
- Emergencies
- Environmental Problems
    - Hostile/Angry People
    - High Activity Levels
    - Facilities Problems
- Budget
- Staffing
    - Under/Over/Improper
    - Untrained
    - Unmotivated/Uncommitted

Resistant to Change
Poor Reaction to Criticism
- Productivity Hard to Measure

The barriers you have identified require action. Identify the ten most important actions you must take on a regular basis to minimize their impact.

- Adjust
- Ask for and Give Data
- Ask Questions
- Assess Results
- Confront Barriers
- Contribute to Group
- Control
- Correct Problem
- Delegate
- Determine Impact
- Develop a Plan
- Develop Personal Goals
- Direct
- Do Alternative Work
- Establish Standards
- Find Source of Problem
- Listen
- Manage Through Participation
- Meet Own Commitments
- Monitor and Assess
- Negotiate
- Organize
- Plan
- Provide Recognition
- Recommend Actions
- Report
- Schedule Time
- Set Priorities
- Staff Effectively
- Take Affirmative Action

- Take Responsibility
- Work from a Written Plan

Finally, identify the ten most important skills, from the list below, needed to do your job. These skills are the transferrable skills that frequently define whether a person will do the job as opposed to the job-related skills that define whether a person can do the job on a technical level.

- Answer Questions
- Attend to Detail
- Be Diplomatic
- Be Persuasive
- Be Self-Expressive
- Be Self-Starting
- Be Self-Directed
- Calm Difficult People
- Coach Others
- Communicate
- Confront Conflicts
- Cope with Stress
- Design/Create/Invent
- Develop Trust
- Empathize
- Encourage Others
- Experiment/Improvise
- Explain Abstract Ideas
- Express Enthusiasm
- Express Ideas
- Follow Details
- Follow Through
- Handle Many Tasks
- Handle the Unexpected
- Influence Attitudes
- Interpret Concepts
- Isolate Data
- Learn Quickly
- Listen Accurately
- Make Decisions

- Observe Behavior
- Observe Things
- Retain Detail
- See Common Threads
- Seek Responsibility
- Solve Analytically
- Summarize Data
- Talk Easily
- Tolerate Repetition
- Treat People Fairly
- Use Intuition
- Use Logic
- Use Numerical Abilities
- Visualize Concepts
- Work with Others

You now have the basis for positive management conflict and management stress. You can link your job and those of the people who work for you into the corporate mission and goals.

Goal Setting

Primary Goal:
To provide the basis, nature, process, and successful implementation of goals

The most consequential skill all ecopreneurs have is goal setting. They know that looking directly for goals, however, is a fool's errand. They are aware the source of all significant goals is need. Needs are the focus of their energies and they put that energy into the achievement of their goals. In truth, goals that are not connected to strong, crucial needs stand only a small chance of being realized, and then only through dumb luck. One final ego-challenge will compare you with an ecopreneur on this issue.

ECO-CHALLENGE—FINAL

Ecopreneurs are aware of their needs and integrate those needs effectively with company and personal relationships.

Rate yourself on the following scale:

3 — I am not aware of the needs that are most important to me at this time in my life and I feel controlled by the circumstances of my job and the context of my relationships.

to

9 — I am totally clear about the needs that affect me most at this point in my life and I have made clear choices and decisions as I have limited any of these needs to achieve a synergy with work and in other relationships.

3	4	5	6	7	8	9

In your words, what statement best describes your rating?

_____

_____

To understand needs is to understand goals. The inventories below will give you an opportunity to examine your company's current needs as well as your own.

In order to establish where your company's focus is in terms of its needs, and also where your focus is in terms of your needs, please complete the following inventory for your company and the one that follows it for you.

Company

Directions: Rank each of the statements in the six situations below as they reflect your company's current conditions and your current conditions (5, for most accurate, and 1, for least). Please use each ranking (5 through 1) only once in each situation.

1. Right now my company is most concerned about
    a. _____ product or service effectiveness
    b. _____ finances
    c. _____ consumer needs
    d. _____ recognition in the field
    e. _____ the future and its possibilities
2. In its words, my company asks its employees to
    a. _____ ensure product/service excellence
    b. _____ attend to financial considerations
    c. _____ operate in strong, effective teams
    d. _____ maintain clear goals and objectives
    e. _____ be loyal
3. In its actions, my company asks its employees to
    a. _____ ensure product/service excellence
    b. _____ attend to financial considerations
    c. _____ operate in strong, effective teams
    d. _____ maintain clear goals and objectives
    e. _____ be loyal
4. The company needs to have
    a. _____ environments free from conflict
    b. _____ enough money to meet its obligations
    c. _____ consumer acceptance reflecting its value
    d. _____ new challenges and growth opportunities
    e. _____ less drain from its physical resources
5. The scuttlebutt reflects a company that is
    a. _____ insecure
    b. _____ not meeting its potential
    c. _____ unsafe to work in
    d. _____ fragmented with no real team effort
    e. _____ unrecognized for its greatness

6. This company will stay in business if it
    a. _____ forecasts and plans the future
    b. _____ increases its financial strength
    c. _____ listens to its consumer
    d. _____ communicates what it is effectively
    e. _____ updates its facilities

Please place your responses below and add the columns generated in that process.

1. a. _____ b. _____ c. _____ d. _____ e. _____
2. a. _____ b. _____ c. _____ e. _____ d. _____
3. a. _____ b. _____ c. _____ e. _____ d. _____
4. e. _____ b. _____ a. _____ c. _____ d. _____
5. c. _____ a. _____ d. _____ e. _____ b. _____
6. e. _____ b. _____ c. _____ d. _____ a. _____

Totals _____   _____   _____   _____   _____
        product   financial   consumer   recognition future
        plant   security   management acceptance growth

You

Directions: Rank each of the statements in the six situations below as they reflect your company's current conditions and your current conditions (5, for most accurate, and 1, for least). Please use each ranking (1 through 5) only once in each situation.

1. Right now, in my life, I am most concerned about
    a. _____ feeling fit/energetic physically
    b. _____ adequate income
    c. _____ association with friendly people
    d. _____ being seen as successful
    e. _____ freedom to be myself

2. Sometimes I wish that I had
    a. ____ a proper diet/weight
    b. ____ a higher level of savings for current needs
    c. ____ relationships with mutual trust and respect
    d. ____ clear and written goals
    e. ____ recognition for my competence
3. I am committed to
    a. ____ being seen as an expert
    b. ____ overall physical health
    c. ____ my growth and personal development
    d. ____ control of my retirement income
    e. ____ mutual consideration and support from others
4. I need to have
    a. ____ environments free from conflict
    b. ____ enough money to do/have the things I want
    c. ____ pay appropriate to my contribution
    d. ____ challenge and new opportunities
    e. ____ limited physical drain on me
5. I often find myself think about having
    a. ____ long-term security
    b. ____ opportunities for developing new skills
    c. ____ a safe, clean environment
    d. ____ real, genuine, and productive teamwork
    e. ____ recognition/respect for my efforts
6. I stay at a job if it provides
    a. ____ growth to my ultimate potential
    b. ____ salary increases reflecting the cost of living
    c. ____ participation in changes affecting me
    d. ____ recognition for the person I am
    e. ____ physically safe and healthy living conditions

Please place your responses below and add the columns generated in that process.

1. a. _____ b. _____ c. _____ d. _____ e. _____
2. a. _____ b. _____ c. _____ e. _____ d. _____
3. b. _____ d. _____ e. _____ a. _____ c. _____
4. e. _____ b. _____ a. _____ c. _____ d. _____
5. c. _____ a. _____ d. _____ e. _____ b. _____
6. e. _____ b. _____ c. _____ d. _____ a. _____

Totals _____   _____   _____   _____   _____
       physical   safety/   relationships   ego   actualization
       health   economics social   recognition potential

What you see in front of you should not be a revelation, either about you or your company. If it is, disregard it. The value of this inventory is in its capacity to enable us to be clear about what is true in our lives. The highest numbers represent the areas of greatest focus or need. It doesn't mean we have no need for the others. It means, at this moment, they are satisfied and to some extent less of a driving force in our lives. This overview, although helpful and somewhat significant in that it verifies the random thoughts we have been having, is only helpful in the broadest of terms. To know you are in great need for recognition or self-actualization can be, in itself, more confusing than not knowing. The first step to becoming clearer and to convert this information about you and your company into a more usable form is to identify the responses that received a five. In doing this you will be defining several clear statements which represent, in your mind, the source of significant goals. By completing the opening phrase of each situation with the most appropriate response, your list could look something like the following:

Your company

1. Right now my company is most concerned about consumer needs.

2. In its words, my company asks its employees to operate in strong, effective teams.
3. In its actions, my company asks its employees to attend financial considerations.
4. The company needs to have consumer acceptance reflecting its value.
5. The scuttlebutt reflects a company that is not meeting its potential.
6. This company will stay in business if it communicates what it is effectively.

You

1. Right now, in my life, I am most concerned about adequate income.
2. Sometimes I wish that I had a proper diet/weight.
3. Sometimes I am concerned with being seen as an expert.
4. I need to have challenge and new opportunities.
5. I often find myself think about having recognition/respect for my efforts.
6. I stay at a job if it provides participation in changes affecting me.

You now have the basis for important goals.

Purpose of goals

Many people consider the purpose of having goals is to provide a sense of direction, like a compass. Other people consider goals to be significant in their energy which draws us to them. I think that neither of these is the most significant reason for goals. I have already suggested the significant impact of goals. They allow us to capture the time we would spend normally in the present worrying about the future.

Judging goal success

The most significant part of all this is that goals, in and of themselves, are not only important for what we say we want. A great deal of the value of goals has to do with what we're willing to do in the present to achieve them. The way you would judge yourself is whether or not you take actions to reach them. Does that mean we were unsuccessful in our goal setting? No, not at all! My sense is, if you have taken actions in the present necessary for you to reach a goal, you have met the expectations in your goal and you are being successful.

Experiencing the goal process

I would like you to experience the goal-setting process before you write your specific goals. This is the goal that I would like you to work through with me.

> "To determine goals for all the significant areas of my life and to be clear on these goals in the next six weeks."

You may have noticed I have assiduously refrained from using the verb *to write* as I have discussed goals. I was once certain only written goals would work. I think written goals are the most powerful but they are not the only way. Three percent of the working population has written goals. They are, not surprisingly, the most successful of any definable group. However, there is about 10 percent of the population that has clear, though unwritten, goals and they are the next most successful. Thinking through your goals appears to be about as powerful as writing them. Being unfocused and confused will keep you in the remaining 87 percent.

The first step in goal setting is to determine a significant need. The second step is to convert that need into a goal. Not by changing the words but simply by changing the need into an intention. The language we should use to express a goal is often confusing to people. It should be expressed in precisely the way you experience the need. Some people need $200,000 a year in income and that is their goal. I need to not have to think about money and that is my goal. Express it as you need it.

Proper weight and diet
Freedom and independence
Recognition for my efforts

The next step is to visualize a time when you want your goals to be realized. If you don't do this, your mind will think you are not really committed to the goal and will occupy itself with other matters.

The next step is to determine some observable and measurable benchmarks that will signify you have reached your goal.

Proper weight and diet
  I will be 40 pounds lighter.
  I will eat nutritional foods.
  I will exercise regularly.
Freedom and independence
  I will determine where I work.
  I will determine when I work.
  I will determine how much I get paid.
  I will travel for fun two months a year.
  I will . . .
Recognition for my efforts
  I will be acknowledged as an expert in _____
  My compensation will reflect my competence.
  I will have the visible signs of success.
  I will be awarded a Nobel prize.

Barriers

The next step in the goal-setting process is to identify the barriers that exist between you and reaching those goals. Unlike the barriers in a performance standard, most barriers in goal setting are internal; some are external, such as time and money, but most are internal. One barrier might be that you don't want to write goals now or you don't feel comfortable with the process. For most people one constant and significant barrier is time, or, more appropriately, the lack of it. Other barriers might be a lack of motivation, being a procrastinator, or a negative attitude toward all of this at this time.

And more barriers

Another barrier is not having anybody in your environment to support you. The support I'm talking about is people who will help you look through and deal with these issues—people who will listen to you, not people who will give advice. Another barrier may be money. You may be unclear about your needs or your stresses. This whole issue of goals may be confusing to you. You may be cynical about goals, thinking they will never make a difference. You may be frightened by the process.

These are some of the barriers that are identified as I work with people in personal effectiveness and goal setting. You may have your own.

Actions

The next step in the goal-setting process is to determine what actions you will take to overcome the barriers. The barrier having to do with time requires certain very specific actions, one of which is to literally schedule time when you're going to do this activity; that is, taking a calendar out, identifying a couple of days or evenings, and saying, "Those evenings, or that day, I'm going to do this." For some of us it may well be that we need to list and prioritize how we want to approach this and then take those issues in priority order. The action is literally to put time on your schedule. Another action is to operate from priorities.

Actions

Your lack of motivation, your procrastination, or your attitude are not going to be dealt with by simply deciding to be more motivated, stop procrastinating, or have a better attitude. If it were that simple, you would have stopped a long time ago. Actions must be discrete and specific. The first action in order to deal with these issues is to make a commitment with yourself to do the tasks associated with your goal every day, such as taking five or ten minutes out of every day to do something on this goal.

Actions

As I mentioned earlier in this program, the only way to maintain a positive attitude, to be positively motivated and overcome issues such as procrastination, is to get tasks done. It isn't to do everything all at once but to do a little bit of something each day and to reward yourself with that feeling of accomplishment and well being. The next action is to recognize that you are inclined to have a poor attitude or to be unmotivated and to see that even though that is true you can either allow it to stop you from doing something in life or it's simply going to be there and you are still going to get what you want from life. Focus on the tasks and these issues will take care of themselves.

Actions

The barrier of support is a significant one because this process works best when you have somebody who will support you going through it. As I said earlier, support means to listen to you, not to give you advice. If you do not have someone in your life right now who will provide support, make a list of those people who are close enough to you whom you might want to contact to give them an opportunity to support you in this activity. Keep in mind you're going to be asking them to be available occasionally to listen to you.

Actions

The issue of money is often a barrier for people. The only thing you can do when money is a problem is either add money to your budget or reduce your expenses. You'll notice that in that context I use the word "budget." The assumption is that you operate with a budget. So the first thing you need to do if you haven't already is to establish a budget. Write down what it costs you to live, what you're expenses are. Then look at the alternatives—reduce your expenses or increase your income.

More actions

Being confused is not a particularly bad place to be. Though you may not see much order, you're looking at your life. It is better than not looking at all. The first thing I would like you to do in order to deal with confusion is not to fight being confused, because if you do, you simply get more confused. Life doesn't require complete clarity. Often we do things and we remain confused. I have discovered that I have had goals I continue to be confused about, but as I worked on them, they became clearer. My goal with regard to the quality of the work life people are experiencing was confusing and eluded me for years. I know I had an important need there. Finally I realized my goal is to have a positive impact on the quality of the work life of every person at work in this country—all 100 million. It became clear I would not be able to reach all of them personally, so teaching and publishing books became essential.

THE ATTITUDINAL LEVEL

The attitudinal issues have to do with your willingness to accept the conditions about the ecology and find the best use of your energies. Your attitude is the most explicit predictor of your success. Your attitude leads to your motivation. Your motivation leads to your behavior. Your collective behavior at work is your performance. Your performance is a function of being productive and your productivity is a function of getting the job done. There is no effort required to have a negative attitude. If you "go with the flow," you will have a negative attitude. The irony is, although it takes no effort to be negative, people with negative attitudes are tired most of the time. It takes a great deal of effort to have a positive attitude. If you say at the beginning of a day it is going to be a great day, you have to make it a great day. In all likelihood, left to its own devices, it wouldn't be a great day. People with positive attitudes know that despite the great deal of effort, you have more energy and you are not tired. The only way to sustain a positive attitude is to keep doing the tasks. Positive attitudes are stimulated by getting things done. I have had the opportunity to discuss career and career-related issues with thousands of people. In that context I have recommended certain actions which are time tested to produce results. These actions relate to such things as a résumé, research, networking, and the like. Because I am extremely positive in my beliefs about individual potential, people generally leave my office turned on to their possibilities. Some of them call my office sometime later and say, "It isn't working." I would say, "What isn't working?" They say, "Everyone wants someone fully trained and no one is interested in me." I would say, "How's your résumé coming? Have you done any research? Who have you networked with in the time since I saw you?" You can guess their response. They would finish the résumé some time soon. They found their library card was out of date. The one person they wanted to start networking with had left on a six-month, around-the-world cruise. We don't get to stay positive if we don't get the job done.

Index

Boldface page numbers highlight discussions of key points.

American work environment, 8
Assessment, 13, 91, 125, 163, 171, 173, 188
Attitude, 1, 8, 10–11, **16–17**, 36, **38–39**, 41, 51, 53, 71–72, 96–97, 119, 127, 141, 155, 172, 178, 190, 192, **201–205**
Authoritative/authoritarian behavior, 20, **113–114**, 118, 121, 125, **127–129**, 131, 133, 175

Behavior, 1, 11–12, 14–15, 19, 22–23, 26, 55, 64, 72, 97, **114–120**, 123, 126–129, 204

Catalyst, **44–45**, 47, 49, 51, 53–54, 56
CEO, 3, 14–15, 17, **19–20**, 23, **25–26**, 28–29, 104, 116, 119–121, **123–133**, 136, 138, 146–147, 178
Change, **1–5**, 7–8, 11, 13, 15, 18–19, **24–26**, 28, 41, 53, 71, 81, **98–101**, 118–119, 123, 135–137, **152–155**, 158–159, 162–163, 181, 184, 190–191, 197, 199

Communication, 8, 36, 67, 95, 106, 118, 125–126, 128–129, 132, 135–136, 151, 167, 170–171, **173–178**, 190
Conflict management, 2–3, 138, 143, 178
Control, 2, 8–9, 13, 20–22, 33, 35, 59, 64, 66, 72–73, 75–76, 82, 85–86, 96, **98–103**, 105, 109, 116, **126–129**, 138, 153–154, 164, 166–167, 176–177, 181, 191, 197
Crisis management, 109–110, 148
Custodial behavior, **113–114**, 118, **129–130**, 133

Demographics, 51

Eco-challenge, 10, 12, 37, 46, 48, 50–53, 55, 59–60, 62, 65, 67, 72, 74, 76, 78, 84–85, 96–97, 100–101, 105, 107, 109–110, 117, 128, 133, 136, 142, 148, 151–154
Ecopreneur, 7–8, **10–12**, 31, 37, 46, 48, 50, 52, 54, 56, 59, 61, 63, 65, 67, 72, **74–78**, 85–86, 93, 97–98,

207

208 *Index*

Ecopreneur *(continued)*
101–103, 106–107, **110–113**, 117, 129, 134, 137, 142, 145, 149, 151, 154–156, 159–160, 165, 170, 176–184, 193–194
Ecopreneurial consciousness, 8
Ecopreneurial technology, 113
Ecostructure, 8
Ego-challenge, 10, 12, 54, 56, 59, 61, 63, 65, 67, 72, 75, 77–78, 85–86, 97–98, 101–102, 106–107, 110–112, 117, 129, 134, 137, 142, 149, 151–152, 154–155, 193–194
Environment, 1–2, 4, **7–9**, 11–12, 17–18, 20–21, 26, 35, 40, 42, **44–47**, 52–53, 71, 82, 87, 119, 121, 127, 129, 138, 144, 149, 152–156, 159, **166–169**, 171, 174, 190, 195, 197, 202

Fiscal management, 30, **44–45**, 53–55, 58, 90

Geographics, 51
Goal management, 183
Goal setting, 193, 200–202
Goal success, 199
Goals, 7–9, 18, 20, 22–23, 26, 33, 37–38, 43, 48, 52, 59, 61, 66–67, 73, **81–82**, 86, 89, 99, 107–108, 110–112, 124, 128–129, 134, 139–141, 145, **147–150**, 152, 154, 160–164, 167, 179–184, 187, 191, **193–195**, **197–202**, 204
Group process, 69
Growth, 22, 55, 57, 61, 66, 78, 80–81, 90–91, 94, 105, **108–111**, 158, 162, 164, 166, 181, **195–197**

Hierarchy of needs, 81
Horizontal management, 105

Ideal company, 10
Individual potential, 81, 95, 145, 205
Integrated management, 77–79

Management behavior, 22, **117–118**, 151, 155, 167
Management communication, 8, 151, 170
Management conflict, 2–3, 8, **69–70**, 75, 77, 79, 113, **138–139**, 143, 178, 193
Management stress, 2, 8, 113, **143–145**, **148–150**, 156, 174, 178, 180, 183, 193
Management style, 2, **113–117**, 118, **130–131**, 135, 138, 167, 178
Management team, 23, 77, **94–95**
Management time, 2–3, 8, 36, 113, 149, 151, 154, **178–184**
Market driven, 4, 49, 62, **104–105**, 107, 115, 139
Marketing, 22–23, 28, 34, 47, 120, 124
Maslow, Abraham, 81
Matrix, 105
Mission, 20, **47–48**, 61–63, **66–67**, 76, 82, 99, 103, 107, **109–112**, 114, 138–139, **148–150**, 158–160, 178–180, 182–183, 189, 193
Motivation, 46, 82, 109, **201–202**, 204

Needs, 13, 22, 25–26, 33, 47, 49, 51, 58, 60, 62, 64, 66–67, 74, 76, 78, **80–84**, 86, 88, 99–100, **103–105**, 107, 109, 111, 117, 119, 124, 131, 133–134, 139, **141–143**, 148, 152, 157, 170, **177–178**, 181, 193–195, 197–199, 202

Ownership, 1, **4–5**, 7, 9, 14, 19, 23, **44–48**, 50–51, 53, 56, 63–64, 66–67, 75, 104, 124, 145, 148, 156–157

Participative/participation behavior, 18, 20, 22, **98–101**, 111, 113–114, 118, 131, 133, **135–137**, 173, 175–176, 191, 197, 199

Performance evaluation, 15, **35–37**, **88–89**, **102–103**, **105–106**, **130–131**, **139–141**, 143, 145, 147, 184

Performance standards, 15, **86–87**, 98, 103, 111, 134, 143, 145, 151, 184, 188, 201

Planning, 20, 61, **66–67**, 94, **108–109**, 111, 137, 148, 160, **178–179**

Politics, 9, **15–16**, **23–24**, 28, 121, 127, 173

Product driven, 30, 34, **43–45**, 47, 49, **51–53**, 60–61, 64, 66, 89, 91, 94, **104–105**, 124, 139–140, 143–144, 146–147, 157, 160, 184, 195–196

Productivity, 9, 12, 15, 23, **29–31**, 45, 60–61, 80–81, 86, **89–93**, 95, 97–100, 102–103, 105, 111, 143, 147, 154, 191, 204

Recognition, 35, 63, 72, 81, 94, 102, 105, 111, 150, 191, **195–199**, 201

Resistance, 33, **98–101**, 106, 135–136

Resource management, 58–59

Self-assessment, 131
Self-employed, 4
Senior management, 19, 21–22, 126, 129–134, 137
Standards, 15, 35, 70, **86–89**, 93, 96–99, 103, 111, 127, 134, **142–143**, **145–147**, 150–151, 158–160, 163, 165–166, 168–169, 184, **188–191**, 201

Stress management, 2, 143–144, 149, 178

Structure, 8–10, 12, 49–50, 73–74, 79, 102–105, 107, 109, 139

Style of management, 104, 114, 129, 131, 133, 136, 170

Success, 1, 3–4, 8, **10–13**, 16–17, 20–22, 26, 29, 35, 40, 42–43, 45–46, 53, 55, 58–59, 65, 69, 71–73, 75, 85, 89, 92, 103–104, 120, 127–128, 132, 139, 143, 148, 150, 152, 154–155, 165–166, 178, 182, 193, 196, **199–201**, 204

Team/team building, 8, 23, 25, 54, **69–70**, **77–79**, 92, **94–95**, 161, 163, 165, 169, 190, 195, 197, 199

Technology, 33, 41, 44, 47, 49, 51, 53, 65, 96, 113, 177, 184

Time management, 2–3, 114, **163–164**, 166, 178–179, 182–183

Turnover, 17, **83–86**, 89, 93, 97, 100–101, 109, 111

Work environment, 1, **7–8**, 12, 42, 44, 87, 153, 156, 174

Work force, 9, 51, 53, 80, **83–85**, 89, 96–97, 99–100, 105, 109

Zero defect, 7